T0023460

Praise for Peter Mayle's

My Twenty-Five Years in Provence

"[A] well-loved writer's contented recap of a life well lived. . . . Mayle set a new course for travel writing."
—*Minneapolis Star Tribune*

"Delightfully quaint anecdotes from the years since Mayle and his wife, Jennie, escaped office life in New York and London in the 1980s for 'a simpler, sunnier life' in Provence. . . . Composed in a uniformly bright and jocular voice, this is a breezy valedictory note for a much-admired writer." —*Publishers Weekly*

"A welcome, if bittersweet, victory lap. The book's final sentences are particularly resonant of a life well lived: 'I must go. Lunch is calling.'"
—*The New York Times Book Review*

"Mayle takes readers back to the idyllic, slow-paced, and occasionally befuddling world that [he] first wrote about in his bestselling memoir *A Year in Provence*. . . . [*My Twenty-Five Years in Provence*] treads delightfully familiar ground for fans who succumbed to the charms of Mayle's first book. The new volume transports readers to the South of France through the eyes of an Englishman who never ceases to marvel at the sunshine, fine food, and sometimes inscrutable culture of his adopted turf."

—Associated Press

"In this final memoir, Mayle returns to the beginning. . . . This is France, so of course food and wine play a large part in his writing. But while Mayle can pen a mouthwatering description of bouillabaisse, what has always drawn readers to his writing are his loving portraits of people, community, and the Provençal way of life." —*BookPage*

"Mayle's mellowest book, touched by the tenderness of a writer summing himself up. . . . Even in moments of majesty, Mayle's puckish humor prevails."

—*The Wall Street Journal*

"One of the most successful and influential memoirists of our era. . . . [Mayle's writings] not only inspired people to explore the French countryside, they encouraged travelers to explore the world *differently*."
—*Toronto Star*

"Peter Mayle may have single-handedly created an American and British obsession with the French region of Provence when he published *A Year in Provence* in 1989. . . . [His] latest book . . . retains the charm of the original. His gentle humor and precise descriptions bring to life a region where time is relative and old ways persist." —*The Providence Journal*

"A warm, sentimental, vicarious glimpse into a life well lived."
—*Canadian Living*

"[An] amusing, pleasantly written, and easily read book."
—*The New Criterion*

"Confirmation that daydreams do come true. . . . Mayle had the gumption to do what many only daydream about: run away to a paradise."
—*Library Journal*

Peter Mayle

My Twenty-Five Years in Provence

Peter Mayle wrote fifteen previous books. He was a proud recipient of the Légion d'Honneur from the French government for his cultural contributions. He died in 2018.

www.petermayle.com

ALSO BY PETER MAYLE

The Diamond Caper

The Corsican Caper

The Marseille Caper

The Vintage Caper

Provence A–Z

Confessions of a French Baker
(with Gerard Auzet)

A Good Year

French Lessons

Encore Provence

Chasing Cézanne

Anything Considered

A Dog's Life

Hotel Pastis

Toujours Provence

A Year in Provence

My
Twenty-Five Years
in Provence

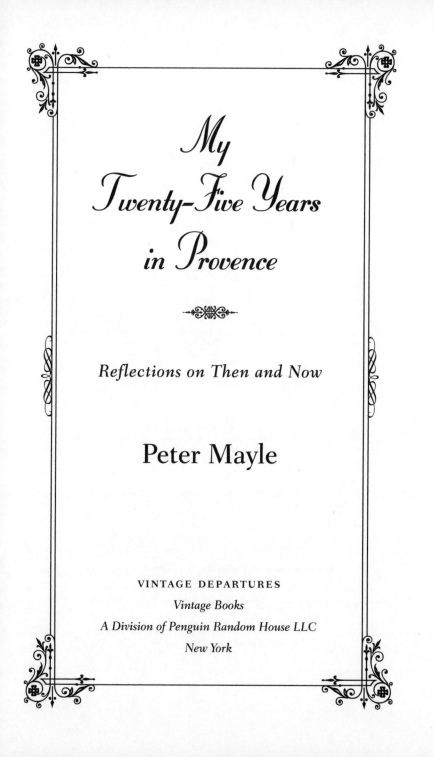

My
Twenty-Five Years
in Provence

Reflections on Then and Now

Peter Mayle

VINTAGE DEPARTURES

Vintage Books

A Division of Penguin Random House LLC

New York

FIRST VINTAGE DEPARTURES EDITION, MAY 2019

Copyright © 2018 by Escargot Copyrights Ltd.

All rights reserved. Published in the United States by Vintage Books,
a division of Penguin Random House LLC, New York. Originally published
in hardcover in the United States by Alfred A. Knopf, a division of Penguin
Random House LLC, New York, in 2018.

Vintage is a registered trademark and Vintage Departures
and colophon are trademarks of Penguin Random House LLC.

The Library of Congress has cataloged the
Knopf edition as follows:
Names: Mayle, Peter, author.
Title: My twenty-five years in Provence: reflections
on then and now / Peter Mayle.
Description: New York : Knopf, 2018.
Identifiers: LCCN 2018001245
Subjects: LCSH: Mayle, Peter—Homes and haunts—France—Provence. |
Provence (France)—Social life and customs. | Provence (France)—
Description and travel. | Mayle, Peter—Homes and haunts—France—
Provence. | BISAC: TRAVEL / Essays & Travelogues. | TRAVEL / Europe /
France. | BIOGRAPHY & AUTOBIOGRAPHY / Personal Memoirs.
Classification: LCC DC611.P961 M35 2018 | DDC 944.9/084—DC23
LC record available at https://lccn.loc.gov/2018001245

Vintage Books Trade Paperback ISBN: 978-1-101-97428-5
eBook ISBN: 978-0-451-49453-5

Book design by Betty Lew

www.vintagebooks.com

Printed in the United States of America
10 9 8

Contents

Contents

My
Twenty-Five Years
in Provence

One

Early Days

*I*t started with a lucky break in the weather. My wife, Jennie, and I had escaped the rigors of the English summer to spend two idyllic weeks on the Côte d'Azur, which according to popular rumor enjoys three hundred days of sunshine a year. But not that year. It rained, hard and often. The beach umbrellas hung in sodden clumps. The *plagistes*, those bronzed young men who patrol the beaches, were huddled in their huts, their shorts soaked. Cafés along the Promenade des Anglais were filled with forlorn parents and fractious children who had been promised a day splashing about in the sea. In the *International Herald Tribune*, there was news of a heat wave in England. As we prepared to leave Nice, we hoped the heat would last until we got home.

A situation like this requires some kind of consolation. We considered going across the border to Italy, hopping on the ferry to Corsica, or making the long drive down to Barcelona in time for dinner. But in the end, we decided on exploring France. Instead of taking the *autoroutes,* we would stay on the smaller secondary roads. Even in the rain, we thought, they would be prettier and more interesting than joining the procession of trucks and caravans on the main highway to the north. And besides, our experience of France had been confined to Paris and the coast. This would be virgin territory.

In those days, long before GPS, we used maps. And one of the few familiar names we found was Aix-en-Provence. There would be restaurants in Aix. There might even be sunshine. Off we went.

The Route Nationale 7, I think, is the French equivalent of Route 66, which the old song taught us was where to go to get our kicks. The kicks on the RN 7 used to be at their height each year in July and August, when most of Paris took what was then the main road down to the south. It, too, had its famous song, performed by Charles Trenet, the lyrics dripping with *le soleil, le ciel bleu, les vacances,* and the promise of wonderful times.

The reality didn't quite live up to the song. The RN 7 is a perpetually busy road, and was filled on that particular day with many of the thousands of trucks that crisscross France, often driven by very large men who look down on passing cars with a faintly menacing air. *Overtake me at your peril,* they seemed to be thinking. *And if you value your life, don't change lanes too suddenly.*

Gradually, the rain was beginning to thin out, and by the time we reached Aix, the gray sky was showing hopeful fragments of blue; to celebrate, we decided to go to the oldest brasserie in town, Les Deux Garçons. Founded in 1792, this is more of a historic monument than a mere bar. Past customers include Cézanne and Zola, Picasso and Pagnol, Piaf and Camus. The terrace overlooks the Cours Mirabeau, the most handsome street in Aix, lined with plane trees and dotted with fountains, the perfect spot to watch the passing crowd. There was a moment when the normal air of conviviality had been disturbed by a shooting in one of the toilets. A vile rumor that the culprit was a waiter who had been deprived of his tip was found to be untrue, and life returned to normal.

Enjoying a glass of *rosé*, we took another look at the map, where we found a scattering of villages on the northern side of the Luberon mountains. This looked promising, and it was more or less on our way back to England. After a proper Provençal lunch of rabbit in mustard sauce and an ultra-fine apple tart, served by a waiter who could have come out of central casting—white apron, generous belly, and memorably luxuriant moustache—we felt ready for any mountain we might come across.

The further we drove from Aix, the more blue sky we saw pushing away the clouds. There was no sun yet, but it was turning into a pleasant afternoon, made even more pleasant by the change in the countryside once we were well away from Aix. It was beautiful, spacious, often quite deserted. Fields of vines and fields of sunflowers easily outnumbered buildings, and what buildings we saw were charming—weather-beaten stone, faded roof tiles, usually shaded by a couple of venerable plane trees or an alley of cypresses. This, as we later discovered, was typical Provençal countryside. We loved it then, and we love it now.

Every so often, the empty fields gave way to a village, with its church tower presiding over a jumble of stone houses. Several of these had the day's washing hanging out of upstairs windows to dry, which we took as a sign that the locals, who are invariably expert weather forecasters, were anticipating the sun. And sure enough, as we were entering what was described on the map as the Natural Regional Park of the Luberon, out it came, bright and optimistic, making everything look sharp and clean, as though the landscape had been etched against the sky. Those gray, rainy days in Nice might have happened on a different planet.

By now, we were getting distant glimpses of the Luberon. It was long and low and its mountains did not seem all that craggy or threatening. They were comfortable mountains. The Luberon even had a road that seemed to go all the way through from the south side, where we were, to the north. We picked up this road outside the village of Lourmarin, and headed north, on what turned out to be the only straight piece of tarmac for several miles. Then came the bends. It was the first time I have ever felt seasick in a car. To make matters worse, the road was narrow, often with a steep wall of rock on one side and a sharp drop on the other. And there was oncoming traffic. Motorcycles were easy enough to dodge, even though they were using the road like a racetrack. Cars could just about pass if we squeezed up against the rock wall. Trailers and motor homes were the challenge, particularly on those bends. We squeezed until we were almost scraping the rock. We sucked in our stomachs and held our breath. Jennie very wisely shut her eyes.

Relief finally came with a flattening and widening of the road, and a sign pointing to an outpost of civilization, the village of Bonnieux. This turned out to be a postcard village, perched on a hill, with ten-mile views across the valley. Using the map, we looked for our next stop, and our eye was caught by something marked in bold type: the *Village des Bories*. What, we wondered, were Bories? Members of a small but privileged tribe, permitted to have their own village? Or perhaps it was a refuge for rare mountain animals? Or even, in these liberated days, a nudist colony? We decided to take a look.

Not a nudist to be seen when we finally reached the village, but an extraordinary collection of small buildings made, without the benefit of concrete, from six-inch-thick slabs of local limestone. These were *bories,* twenty-eight of them, looking a little like giant beehives, built during the eighteenth and nineteenth centuries. There were sheep shelters, oven houses, a silkworm-breeding facility, barns, and granaries—all the modern conveniences of that era, and all very well cared for.

As one often does after a plunge into history, we emerged in need of refreshment. And luckily, it was available just up the road in the village of Gordes. Today, it is a model of rural sophistication, with good hotels and restaurants, boutiques, and, during the summer, a steady flow of tourists. Back then, it was sleepy, almost empty, and astonishingly beautiful, like a film set made from stone.

Gordes dates from 1031, and as we walked across the main square it was easy to imagine that not much had changed since then. Centuries of sunshine had left their mark on the complexion of the buildings, leaving them the color of light honey. Centuries of the *mistral*, the wind that, from time to time, sweeps across Provence, had smoothed the stone surfaces. And, to add to the pleasures of the late afternoon, there was a café on the edge of the square.

We sat on the terrace, with its long-distance views of the surrounding countryside, and I think this was perhaps the moment that the stirrings of change came to us both. It would, we agreed, be a wonderful place to live. We had both done our terms of office duty, working in London and New York for many long years, and we were ready for a simpler, sunnier life.

The sun had begun to drop, and we had to start thinking about where to spend the night. The café waiter sucked his teeth and shook his head. There was nothing he cared to recommend in Gordes, but if we wanted to go to Cavaillon, the nearest large town, we would undoubtedly find a range of suitable amenities.

Cavaillon is the melon capital of France; indeed, the melon capital of the world, if you believe the local melon enthusiasts. It's not a strikingly pretty town, more workmanlike than picturesque, but after Gordes it seemed big and bustling. Here, certainly, we would find a decent meal and a bed for the night.

The hotel was easy. We found it as soon as we came into town: well placed on a main street, slightly shabby, but not without a certain faded charm. The woman at the front desk, herself with a certain faded charm, gave us a smiling welcome.

"We'd like a room for the night, please."

The woman's eyebrows went up. "For the *night*?"

She showed us to a small room in the hotel's main corridor, asked us to pay in advance, and recommended a restaurant two minutes away.

Chez Georges was our kind of restaurant—short menu, paper tablecloths, already busy, with an appetizing whiff of cooking each time the kitchen door swung open. We had, of course, Cavaillon melon to start. It was everything a melon should be, fragrant and juicy. The wine we had ordered was served in an earthenware jug by an elderly gentleman who might have been Georges himself. He suggested that we follow the melon with the specialty of the house, *steak frites*. The steak was excellent, and the French fries were enough to make a gourmet weep with pleasure. They were perfectly crisp, free of any trace of oil or grease, light and satisfyingly crunchy. If this was Provençal cooking, we could hardly wait for the next meal.

But it had been a long day, and bed beckoned. Back at the hotel, we passed a couple of rather furtive-looking men making their way down the corridor before we reached our room, and we had barely closed our door before there was the sound of more activity—a girlish giggle, a burst of masculine laughter, a door being closed very firmly. It sounded as though the other residents, clearly a lively bunch, were having a party.

This went on for most of the night. Doors were banging, footsteps thundered up and down the corridor, and sleep was hard to find. It was some time later that we were told we had spent the night in the local brothel.

$\mathcal{T}wo$

Home Sweet Home

$\mathcal{I}$t is one thing to think about changing countries when you're sitting on a sunny café terrace, and quite another when you return to the real world. Every day after our return to England, Provence seemed more distant; every day, more desirable. At this stage, we didn't even know whereabouts in Provence we wanted to live. If you include the Côte d'Azur (which we don't; it's nothing like the true Provence), the region covers more than thirty thousand square kilometers, from the mountains in the north to the beaches of Cassis and Marseille in the south. So, knowing precious little about our future home, we were at first reduced to daydreaming and reading travel books, which just added to our impatience.

Jennie, at least, did something constructive by enrolling herself in a French class, where she was surrounded by teenage students. I was already an enthusiastic exponent of schoolboy French, with an accent that had inspired a woman in Gordes to say, *"Mais monsieur, vous parlez français comme une vache espagnole!"* At first, I took this as a colloquial compliment, but she had actually been comparing my accent to that of a Spanish cow.

As winter began its muddy march across the damp English countryside, we consoled ourselves with maps, the *Guide Michelin*, and plans to return to Provence in the early summer. This time, we would be more thorough and altogether more businesslike. How much would it cost to live there? Were English refugees made welcome? Did we need official residence permits? Would our two dogs need passports? What about the dreaded French taxes? There were hours of discussion, much of it based on optimism and ignorance. It seemed like the longest winter in living memory, but at last it was over, and we could, mentally at least, put on our shorts and sunglasses. We were ready to go.

We had often noticed that when the English take their cars abroad, they fill them with as much of England as possible: plenty of tea, a favorite teapot, chocolate biscuits, winter sweaters no matter the time of year just in case, a couple of small deck chairs, umbrellas, and *always* remedies for an upset stomach, it being well known that foreigners put funny things in their food.

We tried to keep our car empty, leaving plenty of space for the olive oil and wine that we planned to bring back. One of the delightful distractions when driving through Provence is the number of wine-growing properties that invite the thirsty passerby to drop in for a glass or two. This, inevitably, leads to the purchase of a bottle or two. It is a marvelously pleasant and civilized way to go wine shopping. Whether you stop at an old farmhouse or a miniature Versailles at the end of a two-hundred-yard-long, tree-lined drive, the welcome is warm, helpful, and often delicious.

But first, we had to get there, taking the ferry to Calais and heading south through the vast French countryside. France has more or less the same number of people as Britain, but nearly three times as much land. This is evident when you're driving down from one end of the country to the other; the wide open spaces last for mile after mile, looking as though an army of landscape gardeners has been at work: fields and hedges are neat, fences are well kept, tractor furrows are scrupulously straight. And, more often than not, the landscape is empty: no buildings, no people.

The old saying has it that "*Provence commence à Valence,*" and sure enough, just after passing Valence we began to see a change in the color of the sky and a change in the architecture, with stone walls and terra-cotta roof tiles replacing brick and slate. The sun began to look permanent, and the temperature crept up. Nearly there.

With the help of a friend who had lived in France for several years, we had rented a small apartment just off the main square in Gordes. It was one hundred yards from the café, two minutes from the village baker, with a promising little restaurant next door. And, a rarity back then, there was a phone. Who could ask for anything more?

On our first full day as residents of Gordes (even if only for two weeks), we had two vital missions: finding provisions—both liquid and solid—and a local real estate agent. It was the work of a couple of hours. Or so we thought.

One-stop supermarket shopping was then confined to towns and cities. In the depths of Provence, if you wanted bread, you went to the baker; meat, to a butcher; fruits and vegetables, cheese, wine, detergent and clothespins, each had specialist suppliers, usually experts in their chosen specialty, and always happy to tell you all about it. Then there were the local customers, mostly suspicious ladies who were determined not to be fobbed off with a bruised peach or a wrinkled tomato. Naturally, the shopkeeper would spring to the defense of his wares. There would be much squeezing and sniffing and, if that didn't work, tasting. This would be accompanied by a spirited sales pitch, and eventually the suspicious lady would dig deep into her purse and complete the sale. It was amusing to watch, but it took time—ten minutes for two melons was typical—and by midday we were still a few items short. Alas, everything closed at noon. We had learned our first Provençal shopping lesson: Start early, be patient, and don't be late for lunch.

Finding a real estate agent had its own complications; not scarcity, but the reverse. In almost every village, we found at least one picturesque nook occupied by an *agent immobilier*. Hanging on the wooden shutters outside the office were photographs of the properties on offer. These triumphs of rural architecture would invariably be described as deals *à saisir*, to grab before the next eager buyer came along. The problem was that to our inexperienced and wildly susceptible eyes, everything looked possible: the ruined barn with its roof almost hanging off; the snug little village house that, probably for good reason, had been uninhabited for twenty-five years; a *pigeonnier* that was so decrepit even the pigeons had abandoned it—all the properties seemed ripe for imaginative renovation.

The real estate agents were naturally as enthusiastic as we were, and their language would have made a used car salesman blush. Every photograph we saw had its commentary—a jewel with unlimited possibilities, a dream, a rare and precious opportunity. And not only that. Several times we were exposed to the agents' secret weapons. These, by some fortunate chance, were all people who, for a price, would be delighted to help us. Many were related to the agent. A brother-in-law who was an architect, a cousin who was an electrician, an aunt who was a landscape gardener *extraordinaire.*

Luckily, common sense came to the rescue, and every blandishment was resisted. We reminded ourselves that we wanted a house we could live in, not a five-year project, and so the search continued.

Meanwhile, we were experiencing some of the pleasures and curiosities of village life, and we soon learned that we were a minor local news item. Strangers would stop us in the street to ask if we had found a house yet. One evening we found a friendly old man at the front door. After establishing that we were *les Anglais,* he explained the reason for his visit.

"It is said that you have a telephone. Very unusual in this village."

We did indeed have a phone. "*Ah, bon,*" he said. "I have a son. His wife is expecting a baby, but I have heard no news. I would like to call him."

We showed him the phone and left him to it, anticipating a call of a couple of minutes. Quarter of an hour later, he reappeared, smiling broadly.

"I have a grandson. Three kilos."

We congratulated him. He thanked us, and said he had left something for us by the phone. Sure enough, there was a twenty-centime coin on the table. It was not until we got the phone bill that we found that his son lived in Martinique.

The days were amusing, fascinating, sometimes frustrating. This was mainly due to our struggles with the language, made worse by the Provençal habit of speaking at breakneck speed, accompanied by a distracting selection of tics and gestures, a kind of visual punctuation. Noses would be tapped in a significant manner, indicating the need for discretion; hands jiggled, to hint that what was being said was perhaps not strictly accurate; thumbs were bitten, biceps slapped, earlobes pulled, acrobatic eyebrows waggled. And this was in the course of polite conversation; heaven knows what physical excesses would be involved in a full-blooded argument.

Our house-hunting luck changed at the beginning of the second week, when we met Sabine in her little office in Bonnieux. Unlike the other real estate agents we had met, Sabine listened when we tried to explain what we wanted instead of trying to sell us what she had. Petite and charming, she immediately won our confidence when she warned us of some of the pitfalls of village life, from the nosiness of neighbors to mysterious and long-lived feuds. As outsiders, she said, and especially *foreign* outsiders, we would be the focus of intense curiosity and gossip. It would be good to find somewhere secluded, away from prying eyes and wagging tongues. How did we feel about that?

She was pleased to hear that we agreed with her. And then, as if struck by a sudden blinding flash of inspiration, she smacked the palm of her hand to her forehead, and said, "But of course!" She explained that she had, that very morning, received the photographs of a property that had just gone on the market. It might be perfect.

The photographs were produced. They showed a rambling barn-cum-farm, its mellow stone façade bathed in sunshine, a dog asleep in the shade of a plane tree. You could almost hear the chirp of crickets. It was lyrical, and there was more to come.

Sabine explained that the house was built on the slope of a hill, overlooking an uninhabited valley—a private view, she called it. By now, we were ready to move in. Even the price wasn't enough to put us off; we'd scrape up the money from somewhere. A date was made for us and Sabine to see the property the following afternoon.

The house was everything the photographs had promised, and the private view was the stuff of postcards. The proprietor, an amiable artist, told us to wander wherever we wanted, while he sat in the shade chatting to Sabine. We explored, taking photographs, making notes, finding places for our furniture, and deciding what could be done with the rather primitive kitchen. There would be plenty of time later to talk about money, but for the moment we were giddy with excitement.

This must have been obvious to the proprietor, Monsieur Leconte. Sensing a quick sale, he produced a bottle of *rosé* and told us about some of the property's less obvious charms. In the valley below the house, he said, there was a clump of truffle oaks which, each winter, produced a fine harvest of these magic mushrooms. The slope of the hill behind the house protected it from the *mistral,* the fierce wind that blows in from Siberia, and which is blamed for everything from dislodged roof tiles to attempted suicide. There was an ample private supply of water, it was perfect country for our dogs, and there were no tiresome neighbors to bother us. By the time he had finished his list, we were well and truly sold.

To celebrate, we went that evening to a restaurant that Sabine had recommended in the tiny village of Buoux. She knew Maurice, the owner and chef, and she said we wouldn't be disappointed. We weren't. It was the beginning of a long and delightful series of lunches and dinners eaten outside, in the summer, and in front of the big fireplace in the winter, and I think it's fair to say that we've enjoyed every mouthful over many years.

On this, our first visit, euphoria was the dish of the day. We couldn't believe our luck. It seemed too good to be true.

Which, of course, it was.

Three

Getting Closer

*W*e had sat up until the small hours of the morning, counting our chickens. The following afternoon, we were to have a meeting with Sabine in her office to go through all the details that would-be house buyers need to know before becoming proud owners. Even this, dreary though it might be, was a step forward, and we arrived at the office ten minutes early.

The first hint of trouble was the expression on Sabine's normally cheerful face when she came out to greet us. Mouth set, brow furrowed, she had the look of a woman on her way to a funeral, and she wasted very little time before giving us the bad news.

She had spent a good part of the morning on the phone talking to Monsieur Leconte. There was a problem, she said, with the ownership of the house—or, rather, with part of the house. Did we remember the outbuilding next to the kitchen? Of course we did; we already had plans to knock some walls down and join the two buildings to enlarge the kitchen.

Sabine sighed, and shook her head. Impossible, she said. The outbuilding didn't belong to Monsieur Leconte. It seemed he had lost it during a card game a couple of years earlier. He had tried several times since then to buy it back, but without any luck. To make matters worse, the current owner of the outbuilding said that he intended to leave it to his children. This had destroyed his friendship with Monsieur Leconte and the two men no longer spoke to each other. Unfortunately, said Sabine, stories like this one were not uncommon in Provence, particularly when large families were involved. The problem was that under French law, the children must share equally in most of the proceeds when the parents die, an obligation that is fraught with trouble.

Say, for example, that the three children of Monsieur and Madame Dupont have inherited a fine old house worth two million euros. The oldest of the children, Henri, wants to sell the house and use his share of the money to travel and have fun. His sister Elodie is horrified; she wants to rent out the house and put the money away for her children. His other sister, Nathalie, younger and a little flighty, wants to set up a hairdressing salon and massage business on the ground floor of the house. The result is an ill-tempered stalemate that can last for years, and sometimes for generations.

Sabine, to her great credit, advised us not to have anything to do with the Leconte property. She said we had to be brave and not to worry. She would find a little piece of heaven for us.

Even so, it was a profoundly disappointed couple that prepared to set off back to England, and we needed something to cheer us up. Filling the car with olive oil, *rosé,* and some of the local red wines helped. And, as Jennie said, we could always come over to Provence anyway, and rent while we searched for somewhere to buy. Before that, however, there was the small but vital matter of selling our house in England.

It was an old farmhouse with a thatched roof and sweeping views over the Devon countryside, and the local real estate agent, a languid young man in head-to-toe tweed, pronounced it "super saleable." But when? There was no shortage of prospective buyers. One by one, they loved the house—but several found it too isolated, or were suspicious of what strange creatures might be living in the thatched roof, or admitted that they would feel uncomfortable without neighbors; there was always something. The weeks went by—slow, frustrating weeks.

Salvation finally appeared in the form of an artistic young man who lived with his parrot, Roger. He came, he saw, he agreed to buy. It would take four or five weeks to complete the sale formalities, but we didn't care. We were, or shortly would be, flush with cash. Major progress had been made. We were on our way. We called Sabine with the good news and she said she was sure that something quite *splendide* would come along shortly. We celebrated the evening with a bottle of *Côtes de Provence,* and wine had never tasted so good.

With a short and brutal session of house clearing behind us, we loaded the car to leave. We had decided to furnish more or less from scratch in Provence, taking advantage of the antiques markets and the local artisans, so most of the extra space in the car was taken up with the two dogs and their baskets. Just about everything else had been sent off to be sold.

This time, driving down from Calais, France felt different. Now it was to be our home, and each of us admitted to feeling a touch of apprehension as well as excitement. It's not too hard to do this kind of thing when you're in your twenties, but we were, to put it kindly, mature.

As we left the north and the middle of France behind us there was once again the change in the color of the sky, from pale gray to a thick, cloudless blue. It came like a dose of 100-proof optimism, chasing away the apprehension and turning our thoughts to something practical and sensible, like dinner.

When we reached Gordes, it was glowing in the sunset. Even though summer was just beginning, it was already warm enough to eat outside, and we decided to try the restaurant next door to the apartment we had rented before.

Chez Monique was a little classic, with Madame Monique taking care of the front of the house while her husband, Jules, and his young assistant stayed in the kitchen, where they produced simple, traditional favorites. Unlike many chefs, who constantly tinker with ambitious, complicated dishes in the hope of a Michelin star, Jules was content to stay with what he was good at. The menu was short, and changed daily. The white plates were blessedly free from the artistic smears of sauce that were then becoming fashionable. The wine list was a model of brevity: red, white, or *rosé,* served in generous carafes. We felt very much at home.

We chose a table outside, so that we could bring the dogs with us. When we asked if this was allowed, Monique laughed. *"Mais oui, bien sûr,"* she said. She turned to face the inside of the restaurant, whistled, and out came Alphonse, a majestic Basset hound, who ambled over, sniffed our dogs, and lifted his leg on a nearby lamppost before going back inside to bed.

Monique took our order, coming back at once with a carafe of red for us and a large bowl of water for the dogs, something you're unlikely to get in most Michelin-starred restaurants. All traces of apprehension now gone, we sat back and enjoyed the moment. The last of the sun caught the buildings, giving the stone a honey-colored softness. The café across the square was lively, and we heard snatches of German and English coming from customers on the terrace. Like us, they were early visitors, preferring the warmth of June to the thudding heat of July and August. Unlike us, they would all be going home in a week or two, while we would be staying. It was difficult not to feel smug.

Monique offered to choose what we ate: iced melon soup to start with, she said, would cleanse the palate and alert the taste buds. To follow, she recommended her personal favorite, roast lamb from Sisteron, "the best lamb in France," with flageolets, "haricot beans from heaven." How could we resist?

The melon soup, wonderfully cool and smooth, had been subtly flavored with fresh basil, and by the time we'd finished it, our taste buds were, as Monique had promised, on high alert. They weren't disappointed.

The lamb was pink and tender, the flageolets might have just been picked, and the tiny roasted potatoes were a golden bonus.

There was local cheese and, Jennie's weakness, a tart with thinly sliced apples. Coffee, and a shot glass full of dangerously smooth *marc de Provence,* and we were ready to take the dogs for a stroll. They immediately noticed, as we had, that the air in Provence smelled different and exotic. The lampposts, too, had a certain *je ne sais quoi* that they found fascinating. It had been an evening of discovery for us all. Our life in Provence had started well.

Four

Second Impressions

*B*ack once again in our rented apartment, it didn't take long before the differences between being *les Anglais en vacances* and resident foreigners made themselves felt, and it was a surprisingly good-humored experience. Our attempts at the French language were tolerated, often causing laughter, sometimes provoking replies in pidgin English. These were delivered with much gravity, solemn nods, and finger wagging, with an expectant pause at the end to listen to my reply. This wasn't always easy.

"It is well known to us in France that all English men have a passion for *le cricket*. It is like our *boules, non?* Please explain me the rules of this sport" was my least favorite topic. I would try to oblige, but I could see eyes glaze over once I began to describe the functions on the cricket field of short leg, long on, silly mid off, third man, gully, and second slip. And by the time I explained that a top-class cricket match could last for five days without achieving a result, I knew I had thoroughly confused my audience. It was time for a glass of wine and a change of subject to something simple, like politics.

Our decision to change countries, however, met with universal understanding and approval. Not only was France the finest country in Europe, we were frequently told, but Provence was the finest region in France. Where else does the sun shine for three hundred days a year? Where else do you find the truly authentic *rosé*, sometimes fruity, sometimes dry, a taste of summer in the glass? Where else is goat cheese an art form? And so the list went on, one unique aspect of life in Provence after another.

What was striking about this catalog of blessings was that these enthusiasts weren't trying to sell us anything. They genuinely believed that they were living in one of the most privileged spots on earth, and had no intention of living anywhere else. As we came to know Gordes, we learned of more and more families who had spent their lives there, sometimes in the same house, for generations. Their collective memories went back a hundred years or more. They were like living history books.

This seemed to produce amiable people with a relaxed temperament who took life slowly, avoiding the modern habits of pressure and speed. Naturally, they distrusted the government—*les imbéciles de Paris*—and became a little morose if it rained for more than two days, but on the whole they were cheerful and content. As we found, this was catching. Did it really matter if the occasional pressing chore was postponed in favor of lunch? Time was elastic; there was always tomorrow.

Together with this leisurely approach to life, or perhaps because of it, we found that people were noticeably more polite than we were used to. Handshakes and the kissing of cheeks—sometimes twice, sometimes three times—were obligatory, even if you saw those same people every day. And there was always a moment or two put aside for gossip.

Other first impressions were not always so agreeable, and the French obsession with official bits and pieces of paper was a recurring irritation: we were told to keep such vital national security treasures as our electricity bills, doctors' prescriptions, tax declarations, phone bills, and bank statements for at least two years, sometimes five, and occasionally ten. After only a few years of residence, we thought seriously about renting filing space in a neighbor's garage. (It comes as an anticlimax to admit that, during more than twenty years, we have never been asked to reveal anything—not even our highly sensitive electricity bills.)

Having been impressed by the everyday politeness of the French, it's only fair to mention an aspect of French life where good manners, patience, and civility take a very distant back seat: this is the ancient tradition, undoubtedly invented by the English, of the queue. The French are ingenious and persistent in their determination not to stand in an orderly line and wait their turn. They jostle, they creep, they sidle, or they pretend to be joining a dear friend who happens to be standing at the front of the crowd. I even know of a sprightly old lady who never goes to market without a crutch, otherwise never used, which she wields like a weapon to clear away anyone in her path to the front.

But these aggressive habits, taking place as they do among pedestrians, can't compare with the furious dramas that unfold once the Frenchman gets behind the wheel of his car. His perilous efforts to overtake on a blind bend and to drive six inches behind you are exciting enough, but they are nothing compared with the full range of emotions on display when he is trying to grab a disputed parking spot. He blasts his opponent with a fusillade from his horn. He winds down his window so that his bellowed protests can be more easily heard. Finally, he gets out of his car, much to the noisy annoyance of those trapped in the traffic jam he has caused by blocking the cars behind him, and continues to rant, his arms waving, his face turning puce. By now, drivers from the cars behind him have joined in, horns blaring, and the losing driver has to concede defeat before the local gendarme arrests him for causing a public nuisance. If, as sometimes happens, the contest has occurred in front of a sidewalk café, the loser is often consoled by a round of applause from the café's customers.

Distractions like this can turn a quick trip to the baker's to buy croissants into an entertaining half hour, and we were finding that our old efforts to be organized and punctual were gradually disappearing. We could never pass a game of *boules* without stopping to pick up tips on technique: the narrowed eyes taking aim, the crouch, the graceful swing of the arm, the release of the *boule*—it was like some kind of rural ballet. And then, of course, would come the arguments. The players would gather round the *boules* to see who had landed closest to the *cochonnet* (literally, a piglet, but here the name is used to identify the target ball). Reasoned debate would quickly give way to claims and counterclaims. A tape measure would be produced in the hope of settling the argument, but just when it seemed that a scrap was inevitable, the matter would be resolved and hostilities would cease in favor of a beer in the bar. Cricket was never like this.

In between distractions, our search for somewhere to live permanently continued, a mixture of frustration and enjoyment. It was also an education in the wily ways of people with a house to sell. Without exception, they were supreme optimists when describing their precious properties. A sagging roof and shutters hanging off their hinges were *"pittoresque."* Ceilings so low they would make a dwarf duck were *"intime."* Tiny, dank kitchens with equipment that belonged in a museum were *"traditionnelle."* In fact, most of these properties hadn't been lived in for years, but had been inherited when the previous owners had died. Even so, it was hard to imagine making a home in some of the old relics we saw.

After several months, our luck finally changed. We found a house on a hillside, with several thousand acres of the Luberon Natural Regional Park at the end of the back garden, a modest vineyard, and the fine old stone village of Ménerbes two minutes away.

Our first night was spent, as first nights in new houses often are, with little more than a bed—some furniture would soon arrive from England—but we were too delighted to notice. The dogs were in heaven after their first walk in their private forest. Ménerbes seemed to be a very pleasant village. The house had a pool. There were no close neighbors to worry about. It was home sweet home at last. Now we really were residents of France.

I had occasional urges to write a novel, but something always seemed to prevent me from disturbing the typewriter. Provence had far too many distractions, and two of them were very close to home: our nearest, although quite distant, neighbors were Faustin and his wife, Henriette, whom we had inherited from the previous owners of the house. They had a long-standing agreement to take care of our vineyard, which they did with great diligence. Almost every day, we could see Faustin driving to work on his tractor. In his spare moments, he also gave us an insider's education in the cultivation of the grape and its slow progress into the wineglass. We learned to prune, we discovered how well old vine roots burned in our fireplace, and we had the thrill of tasting our first bottle of wine grown on the premises. (It would never win any awards, but it was *ours*.)

Every season, it seemed, brought its own fascinating reason not to settle down and work. The typewriter accumulated dust, and I was becoming more and more adept at ignoring pangs of guilt—something I now know most writers manage to master at some point in their careers. The *vendanges* came, the grapes were picked, and Faustin put away his tractor. The tourists had gone, and the countryside had suddenly become noticeably emptier. Winter was in the air.

But while villages and vineyards were settling down to their annual hibernation, the forest was humming with activity. The hunting season had started, and no hare, red-legged partridge, or wild boar would be safe until the season had ended in January.

The hunting day got going around seven in the morning, with an opening salvo timed to shock us awake every Sunday. The howls of excited hunting dogs, let loose after a summer in kennels, added to the sound effects, with an extra contribution from our own dogs—a rustic lullaby that went on until lunchtime. Sad to say, periods of silence only occasionally interrupted the gunfire. There were usually about a dozen hunting deaths each year in France, and sometimes more than two hundred accidents that required a trip to the hospital. Recently, a hunter trying to shoot a hare hit his own brother in the leg. Another hunter mistook his son for a partridge. And, in the most implausible case of mistaken identity, an eighty-two-year-old hunter fired at a couple of walkers, mistaking them for a pheasant.

These statistics suggested that walking our dogs in the woods every day was a somewhat risky habit, and one that demanded precautions. We fitted each dog's collar with a heavy-duty, extra-loud hunting bell, and I took pains to make as much noise as possible when making my way through the woods—snapping branches, shouting to the dogs, and cursing loudly from time to time.

This seemed to work, and I very rarely came across a hunter. One I remember bumping into—a small, khaki-clad figure, his bandolier bristling with cartridges—seemed to be a great deal more nervous than I was. As I came closer, he raised his rifle to the port arms position and took a step backward.

"Are those dogs safe?" he asked, taking a firmer grip on his gun and another step back as they came up to investigate him. I resisted the impulse to tell him that they were trained only to attack armed men, and reassured him. Even so, he was clearly irritated that I was trespassing on what he considered to be his personal patch.

"What are you doing here?" He glared at me, shaking his rifle ominously.

"I live here," I said. "How about you? Where do you live?"

This was not a subject he wished to discuss. He stumped off down the path, probably wishing he had shot first and asked questions afterward.

I was pleased to discover another kind of hunting that winter—quieter, much less dangerous, and potentially very profitable. Neither guns nor bullets are required, but there is one essential item of equipment: a dog with a keen sense of smell, a golden nose. But it needs to be a wise old nose that has been trained to detect and unearth one of the most mysterious and expensive mushrooms in the world: *Tuber melanosporum*, the black truffle.

Despite many attempts, it seems that so far there is no way that cultivated truffles can be made to taste as good as the truffle that has grown naturally. And since they grow where they want, around the roots of certain trees, truffles are extremely difficult to find. Hence the dog, the mystique, and the high prices. In 2014, a single large white truffle (Italian, alas) was sold at auction by Sotheby's for more than $60,000, and the current price for more regular-sized black truffles is around $1,000 a pound. Are they worth it? Or is it merely an extrovert's way of putting his money where his mouth is?

We're lucky enough to live in an area where truffles grow, and can often buy them, at a fraction of the Parisian price, from the man who dug them up. And so a regular winter treat is the truffle in its various forms: slipped into an omelet, grated over pasta, or sliced in a risotto. And then there is the most self-indulgent truffle recipe of all, which a friend claims is the closest thing on earth to having heaven in your mouth. You start with a generous slice of *foie gras,* and place it on a sheet of tinfoil. You then place your truffle on the *foie gras* and put it in the oven, where the truffle gradually sinks into the melting *foie gras.* The complex, slightly earthy taste of the truffle and the unctuous coating of *foie gras* may put you off hamburgers forever. *Bon appétit!*

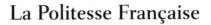

Five

La Politesse Française

*F*or many people who haven't spent much time with them, the French have a less than welcoming reputation: aloof, a little prickly, and definitely not the sort to hug strangers. Like many social myths, this one is not at all reliable. The French are as human as the rest of us, but they come equipped from childhood with what is sometimes seen as a barrier rather than a civilized way of life—the habit of politeness.

This is rare enough in the modern world to be considered a little odd. There was a time in the UK when "Manners maketh man" was widely observed as a useful guide to behavior, but this has long since gone, to be replaced by a slapdash informality. Not so, however, in France, and the difference, to a couple of newly arrived foreigners like we were twenty-five years ago, was striking.

The first thing we noticed was the necessity of

physical contact. Its simplest form was the manly handshake, but that depended on the hand being free. If it was carrying something, the burden had to be put down so the hand was available for shaking. If that wasn't possible, an elbow could be extended; failing that, the last-resort little finger might be presented. I have sometimes passed scenes on the street that might have come from a contortionist's warm-up routine, but appearances aren't important. The essential is to touch. Even with builders, gardeners, and others with work-stained hands, you are offered a wrist—a clean wrist—to shake.

This is just as important among the ladies as it is among men, although slightly more complicated, as it involves multiple cheek-kissing. The standard formula is one kiss on each cheek, taking care that there is not a clash of noses during the change from one side to the other. But this is for traditional kissers. The number rises to three between close friends, and in Aix, where there is a large and affectionate student population, four kisses are quite normal.

Kissing between men, once regarded by British visitors as wildly exotic, barely raises an eyebrow nowadays. I have a friend who says he can tell with his eyes closed when men kiss. He claims to be able to hear the faint rustle of stubble against stubble.

But there is more than kissing to French *politesse*.

It also dictates how people talk to one another. The simple word "you" becomes nuanced and subject to its own rules. There are three words in French for "you"—*vous, tu,* and *toi*—and each has its particular use. *Vous* is the most formal, to be used between people who have just met, or who are separated socially by their position. If the relationship should become friendly, *vous* can be replaced by *tu,* or occasionally *toi,* for added emphasis, as in *Tais-toi*—"Shut up."

There are, of course, exceptions, my favorite being the ex-president of France who persisted in addressing his wife as *vous* even after forty happy years of marriage, when you would have thought a level of intimacy might have been established. But on the whole, the rules are followed. And nowhere more carefully than when following the cast-iron rules of *bonjour.*

This is one of the most valuable words in the language, a verbal passport that helps to put the French world at ease. Forget to use it, and you risk being ignored, or taken for an ill-mannered—or, perhaps worse, arrogant—foreigner. It is even one of the few words to have a price put on it. There used to be a café in Paris that offered this discount for good manners when ordering: Coffee, 2.50 euros. Coffee + *bonjour,* 2 euros. Coffee + *bonjour* + a smile, 1.50 euros. Waiters in restaurants also appreciate being treated like people, and *bonjour* is a good place to start.

Small physical acts of politeness, almost extinct elsewhere, have managed to survive, too. It is not uncommon to see a man stand up when a woman enters a room, to hold open a door to let her pass through before him, or to defer to her in the choice of wine at dinner. (Though this last one is rare.)

Is any of this useful and important, or is it all merely a leftover from more leisurely times? I've become used to it over the years, and I think life would suffer greatly without it, because it is not just a set of social trimmings; these are simple expressions of respect and consideration for others. They make everyday existence more pleasant, whether you're buying a *baguette* or meeting someone for the first time.

There are two notable exceptions to this agreeable state of affairs: the first is the abrupt personality change that takes place as soon as the French get into their cars, when consideration for others takes a back seat.

Normally mild-mannered men and women become impatient, often aggressive, horn blowers and suicidal overtakers, given to yelling their disapproval at the driving ability of anyone in their way, anyone who has taken a precious parking space, and anyone who is driving too slowly. The best response to this is not to react, but to stare straight ahead.

Infuriating, and effective.

The second exception is the queue. I think the problem here is that the queue, in its very early days, was treated as a primitive contact sport without any rules, and nothing much has changed. Women are far better in queues than men. They are more cunning, more ruthless, and more determined, seeing opportunities for pushing in and queue jumping that most men wouldn't dare attempt.

Whenever we go to England, I'm struck by the docile behavior of English queues after the rough-and-tumble of Provençal housewives, and once I actually saw a man give way in an English queue to an anxious woman. Perhaps *la politesse anglaise* is still thriving after all.

Six

Learning French, Inch by Inch

*T*he best way to learn French is to have a partner who is both fluent and patient. Failing that,
you have to muddle along as best you can with phrase
books, the local newspaper, television, and stumbling
exchanges at the post office and with the butcher.
Unless, of course, you are lucky enough to find a good
teacher. This happened to me quite by chance one
Sunday morning, when I was negotiating with the
baker to buy some bread, and a croissant for Jennie.

"Une baguette et une croissant, s'il vous plaît."

At once, I heard a voice behind me say, *"Non, non,
et non."*

I turned around to see the man behind me in
line: a small, gray-haired man wearing small, round
spectacles, his index finger wagging energetically. I
must have looked puzzled enough to encourage an
explanation.

"C'est LE croissant. Masculin."

"Excusez-moi, monsieur. Je suis anglais."

"Ah, bon? I speak English." He held out his hand. "Farigoule."

"Mayle." We shook hands, I picked up the baguette and *le croissant* and turned to leave, but Monsieur Farigoule hadn't finished. "Wait for me outside," he said. "We will have coffee." He looked at his watch. "Or perhaps an *apéritif.*"

We settled down at our table, and Monsieur Farigoule opened the proceedings. "I get very little chance to speak English with an Englishman," he said, "and so I am going to make the most of you."

Which he did, for nearly an hour, speaking good, charmingly accented English, pausing only to order more *rosé* or to check with me that he had used a word correctly. He was, he told me, recently retired from his job as an English teacher at a local school, and was finding retirement a little tedious. The level of intellectual discussion in the village was inadequate, and he was already bored with spending his days tending his small garden. "The brain is like a muscle," he said. "It must be exercised or it will wither. Now tell me: What are you doing to improve your French?"

I looked at him. I wanted to learn French. Here was a professional teacher with plenty of spare time. It wasn't a difficult decision. We agreed to meet each week. Monsieur Farigoule would organize what he called a curriculum. There would be homework. My French, as Farigoule put it, would "blossom like a flower in springtime." As our glasses were emptied and refilled, it became clear that he was extremely knowledgeable about the local wines, knowledge which he promised to share with me. I was delighted. I would have not only a *professeur personnel* but also an experienced palate to guide me through the confusing selection of wines to drink, wines to keep, and wines to avoid.

Jennie, who had just acquired her own teacher, was almost as pleased as I was. Together, we would escape the Anglophone club of expatriate English speakers who resolutely cling to their native tongue. As a first step, we would start speaking French to the dogs.

At one of our early weekly meetings, Farigoule asked me if I had retained what he had said the previous week, which I had. French, he had told me, was not only poetic, romantic, beautiful, and in every way superior to other languages. It was also *logical,* an admirable addition to any language. Adjectives had to agree with nouns. Verbs had to be at the same time precise but flexible. And, one must never forget the fundamental importance of gender. Here, he gave as an example France's favorite phrase. How dull and flat it would be if it were simply *"Vive France,"* and how much more stirring and elegant it became with the addition of France's gender, which was naturally and logically feminine.

I asked him if there was an officially authorized body in charge of gender labels. When a new word crept into the language—e-mail, for instance—who was responsible for deciding whether it should be *un* or *une*? Was this a government matter, supervised by a minister in charge of such things? Or was it the Académie Française, which would normally have the last word on the French language?

I was not really convinced by Farigoule's insistence that French was entirely logical. Language evolves with popular usage, which often ignores logic, and I wanted to see if I could find an example to test Farigoule's theory. I reached for the dictionary and started searching for gender irregularities.

After half an hour, I was beginning to think he was right after all, and that logic reigned supreme. And then, tucked in the dictionary between *vagabondage* and *va-et-vient*, I came across what I was looking for: *le vagin*, the vagina, that indisputably feminine possession—and here it was, presented as though it had changed its mind and become masculine. Where was the logic in that? Where was gender accuracy, so crucial to the French language? And why not *la pénis*? I could hardly wait for the next weekly meeting.

Farigoule was not in the least surprised, nor did he think the choice of gender was illogical. To support his view, he delivered a detailed justification, which included grammatical and biological reasons why the vagina was somehow inevitably masculine.

The following week, I presented to him another discovery. In France, there are 100,000 words in current use; in the UK, that figure is 171,476. Advantage English, or so I thought. But no. According to Farigoule, French is so much more nuanced than English that it doesn't need all those extra words. And then, as he warmed to his task, he started to quote examples from French literature. Eventually, I had to stop him in mid-nuance, pleading a headache.

Luckily, there was no shortage of other, less academic teachers—not as well qualified as Farigoule, perhaps, but certainly experts in nonacademic areas, particularly the language of gestures. I had become fascinated by the physical aspect of French conversations that I had noticed in cafés—the way in which fingers, hands, arms, eyebrows, and sound effects were used to emphasize or clarify what was being said. This seemed to me an important part of learning the language, and a great deal more fun than the correct use of the subjunctive tense.

My first unwitting teacher was Raymond, the *postier,* who came to the house every morning to deliver the mail and, when pressure of work permitted, to have a cup of coffee and gossip. One morning I gave him a letter destined for London, and asked him if it would get there by the end of the week. He nodded and said, *"Normalement, oui."* But I noticed that one hand, held palm down at waist level, was rocking back and forth energetically. I asked him if this signaled a problem.

"Not if everything goes well," he said, and went on to list a few possible causes of delay, starting with the unreliable quirks of the English mail service. So the quivering hand could also be translated as "With a bit of luck" or even "Who knows?" It was shorthand for a lack of certainty, a warning not to take the spoken word literally. I've subsequently come across this silent disclaimer hundreds of times, most often when deadlines are discussed.

The nose plays a versatile part in French sign language. When tapped in a significant manner by an index finger, it can mean that the speaker knows what he's talking about; that what he says should be taken seriously; that this particular conversation is just between the two of us; and variations of all these. When the index finger is curled around the end of the nose and moved back and forth, it's a sign of intoxication (frequently seen in bars and cafés). The hands themselves rarely stop moving—tapping, squeezing, spread wide in disbelief or chopping the air in emphasis—and I have often felt almost physically exhausted after a quiet chat about rugby with my friend Patrice.

Then there is the most aggressive gesture of all, not to be used in polite company. It is an expression of such extreme irritation and contempt that mere words are not violent enough. Instead, one arm is extended toward the object of your displeasure, and the other hand comes across to slap into the bicep. It is the physical equivalent of "**** you!," and is widely used in traffic jams.

Finally, there is the shrug. There was a time when the world saw this as typically French. In those days, reacting to circumstances that would make the Frenchman shrug, the Englishman would put his hands in his trouser pockets, the Italian would smack his forehead with the palm of his hand, the American would pick up the phone to call his lawyer, and the German would lodge a complaint with the chancellor. But nowadays, the whole world has learned to shrug, although I still think the French do it best. With a good, eloquent French shrug, you can not only see what it means, you can almost hear the words that go with it.

Seven

---◆❖◆---

Dinner at the Élysée Palace

*A*fter hundreds of years of name calling, squabbling, and war, the French and the English finally decided that enough was enough, and that it was time to be friends. This prompted the Entente Cordiale, an agreement signed on April 8, 1904, that formalized a new, more amicable relationship between the two countries. It worked. For example, millions of Britons take their annual vacations in France, and there are now 400,000 French residents of London.

By April 2004, the *entente* was still thriving, and the president of France, Jacques Chirac, organized a dinner party to mark its one hundredth anniversary. As you might imagine, this was no ordinary event. For a start, there were to be two hundred guests, including the Queen of England and her husband, Prince Philip, Duke of Edinburgh, as well as captains of industry, senior politicians, and stars of stage and screen. And me.

You may quite rightly ask how someone like me came to be included among this collection of the famous and celebrated. I think there were three possible reasons. First, I was English; second, I had chosen to live permanently in France; and third, I had written a book praising the pleasures of life in Provence. I was a very minor living example of the Entente Cordiale.

Even so, it was a shock when the invitation arrived. And what an impressive piece of work it was—large, thick, and white, with the most elegant black script, and there, at the top, my name written as I had never seen it before. I imagine it was the work of the president's personal calligrapher: with exquisite twirls and flourishes, the kind of writing you might see on banknotes of the very highest denomination. Pasted on the back of the card was a more workmanlike series of instructions telling guests to arrive at 55 rue du Faubourg Saint-Honoré by seven forty-five at the latest, armed with the invitation and proof of identity. It was to be the first time I needed my passport to be allowed to go in to dinner.

There were also suggestions about what should be worn, including *uniforme,* if you were fortunate enough to have one. The rest of us men were expected to wear suits, and here was a minor problem; I still possessed a suit, but I hadn't worn it for at least ten years. I took it out of its bag and considered it. The color, black, was very suitable for an evening out. The jacket still fitted perfectly, but the trousers seemed to have shrunk, and it took a few hours of careful adjustment before I could be confident about bending over or sitting down.

The great day arrived, and I was steered into an area where the guests were to wait before joining the presentation line. I looked around, hoping to see a famous face, but no luck. I was surrounded by dignified, well-dressed, but, for me at least, anonymous men. Not a lady in sight.

The presentation line began to move forward toward the distinguished welcoming committee: the Queen and Prince Philip, and President and Madame Chirac. When my turn came, I was announced by a liveried footman, and greeted by the Queen, who seemed to be genuinely pleased to see me, a graceful knack that she must have perfected over millions of handshakes. After Prince Philip and the Chiracs extended their hands to me, another liveried footman led me away, and I had a moment to appreciate the surroundings.

The Élysée Palace has been the official residence of the president of the republic for more than 150 years, and the assorted presidents haven't skimped on comfort and decor: chandeliers, priceless carpets, paintings on the ceiling—no expense has been spared. Nor have they held back on refreshments for their many guests, whose bar bill is about a million euros a year.

All two hundred of us were to dine in the huge and sumptuous *salle des fêtes,* where each place was equipped with a glittering forest of crystal glasses, a small armory of silver cutlery, and more liveried footmen hovering discreetly in the background. Looking at the hundred meters or so of table settings, I felt considerable sympathy for the kitchen brigade faced with all that washing up.

Almost opposite me were three faces I recognized from their work in music and films: Jane Birkin, Charlotte Rampling, and Kristin Scott Thomas. They looked delightful. In fact, they looked like just the kind of ladies who would welcome the chance to pass a few pleasant moments with a writer. Unfortunately, they were on the other side of an extremely wide table, well out of conversational range. I was forced to try again with the captains of industry on either side of me.

Meanwhile, course after course was served, and glass after glass was topped up. It was all excellent, and beautifully presented, but I wondered if, as a break from the innumerable banquets that she was obliged to attend, the Queen ever longed for steak and French fries or a plate of pasta.

Dinner was drawing to a close. We had eaten well, the speeches had been brief and elegant, and it was time to think about going home. But the highlight of my evening was yet to come.

I signaled to the nearest liveried footman to ask for directions, and quickly found myself in the marbled splendor of the men's room. It seemed empty at first. And then I saw a tall figure making his way toward the door; Prince Philip was about to pass within two feet of me. We nodded to one another, as gentlemen do in these circumstances, and then he was gone.

I was still recovering from the moment when I returned to my place, and noticed that my liveried footman was looking at me intently. He came over, and bent to whisper in my ear.

"Excusez-moi, monsieur, mais la porte est ouverte." He nodded down toward my lap, and I saw that he was quite right. I had forgotten to do up my fly. No wonder I've never been asked back.

Eight

❦

Nostalgia Is Not Always
What It Used to Be

*M*emory is at its best when it's selective, when we have edited out the dull, the disappointing, and the disagreeable until we are left with rose-colored perfection. This is often quite inaccurate but usually very comforting. It can also be fascinating to revisit. Was it really like that? Were we really like that?

During the past twenty-five years, we have occasionally given in to the temptation of slipping back into the past and comparing it with the reality of today. Most of the time, we've been delighted to find little change; even some of the people we remembered as interesting old characters are still there—by now, human antiques, but perhaps more interesting than ever.

There have, of course, been less rewarding results, where today is nothing like it was yesterday, and we've noticed that village cafés are often the victims. Because they are usually in the center of the village, they are often seen as prime sites for selling something more profitable than beer, wine, and cups of coffee. Boutique fever takes over, and bright little stores with even brighter clothing replace café terraces and dimly lit bars.

What is sometimes worse is when the café itself has decided to join the rush to the new with a thorough renovation. The terrace itself may have survived, but the faded wicker chairs and round, metal-rimmed tables that have served it well for twenty-five years have been replaced by plastic tables and chairs, often in lurid colors that sit uneasily in their surroundings of a weathered stone village. Inside the café, it is *encore plastique,* with the sole, massive reminder of old times being the battered zinc bar.

The renovators have also been busy in local restaurants, with mixed results. One of our early favorites was a small, charming place set in the courtyard of a modest eighteenth-century house. It featured paper tablecloths, with one corner used by the waiter to scribble down a record of what you had just ordered. The menu was short, and changed each day. The food was simple, fresh, and excellent. The wine list was no bigger than a postcard, and the wines were all made by growers known to the chef. It was too good to last, and it didn't. After years of working in one of life's more demanding occupations, the chef and his wife took a well-earned retirement, and the restaurant was sold. A sad loss.

The first sign that the new owners were about to change what they had just bought was the platoon of builders who had moved in, shipped out the old restaurant furniture—those comfortable, creaky chairs and slightly wobbly tables—and put up a notice on the courtyard door with the ominous warning that a *rénovation totale* was taking place. Our hearts sank. But, ever hopeful, we decided to come back and take a look when it had been done.

Two steps inside the courtyard, it was already obvious that a great deal of money had been spent. The chipped flagstone floor was now polished tiles, thick white cloths covered each table, the cutlery was heavy and gleaming with newness. The menu was longer, the wine list more imposing. But by far the most dramatic change was the senior waiter. Gone was the chef's wife, in her apron and slippers, and in her place a smooth middle-aged gentleman who was a symphony in classic black and white—black pants, black waistcoat, black bow tie, and starched white shirt. His youthful assistant, smiling and immaculate in her black dress and blond chignon, hovered behind him.

The chairs were elegant and comfortable and the food was fine, although a little too elaborate for our liking. Like so many of his colleagues, the chef had discovered foam, which he used to disguise perfectly good cooking. There was even a separate course that consisted of nothing but foam, served halfway through the meal, and tasting like a dessert that had lost its way. All in all, here was a perfect example of a restaurant that would have been more at home in Paris than Provence. And maybe that is where it's gone; after one season, with the visibly tense waiter, it was replaced by yet another boutique.

But small disappointments like this are more than made up for by the most welcome change of all: the local wines.

When we first arrived here, there was an unkind assessment of Provençal wines, particularly *rosé,* that was popular among the visiting self-styled connoisseurs. Their considered opinion, delivered with a superior smile, was this: "Provençal wines? No sooner made than bottled; no sooner bottled than drunk; no sooner drunk than pissed away." Anyone saying that today would be sent to the bottom of the tasting class and have his corkscrew confiscated.

Wine has been made here in Provence for 2,600 years, and there have been intervals, sometimes of a hundred years or more, when standards have slipped. Now, the wines of Provence regularly receive medals, and are taken seriously all over the world by those who know what they're drinking. The reds are full and subtle and the whites are crisp, but it is Provençal *rosé* that has seen the most dramatic surge in popularity, and for very good reason.

First, its appearance is attractive. Not quite white and not quite red, its color has occasionally been described embarrassingly as "blush." This was often heard in the days when *rosé* had a rather frivolous reputation—a picnic wine, something to be knocked back at lunch before tottering off for a siesta.

Then there's the taste—fresh, clean, slightly fruity, and very versatile. It goes as well with fish and chicken as it does with salads and spaghetti. It is an ideal *apéritif,* too well mannered to overpower the meal that follows. And it's a wonderfully practical wine that doesn't need to be nursed in the cellar for years before it's fit to drink. You can chill it in the refrigerator or in a bucket of ice cubes, but in Provence you will often see ice cubes bypassing the bucket and going straight into the waiting glass. In other words, it is a wine without pretension. But how did it become what it is today?

I believe that much of the credit should go to the Provençal farmer. Traditionally, the small farmer with a few acres of vines concentrated on making the solid, workmanlike red wine that his father and grandfather had produced. We used to live in a house surrounded by vines, which our neighbor Faustin took care of for us. Every year, he would come up the drive on his tractor to deliver a couple of cases of his red wine. It was not exactly vintage claret, but we enjoyed it very much.

During one of his visits, I decided to ask him a question I had been wondering about for some time: Had he ever thought of making a *rosé*?

He got down from his tractor, took off his battered tweed cap, scratched his head, and leaned against one of the tractor's huge back tires. "That's what they drink down on the coast," he said. "It's not *sérieux*. There's not much call for it up here." And that was that. He offered no recommendations, and no suggestions as to where we could find *rosé* locally, although he did offer us a bottle of his homemade *marc de Provence*—guaranteed, he told me, to grow hairs on my chest.

It was not until the following summer that our researches into wine made any significant progress. Two friends had been spending a few days on the Riviera, and we invited them to stay the night with us before starting their long drive back to London.

"Here's a little something to go with dinner," they said, presenting us with half a dozen of the most elegant bottles we'd seen for months—graceful, amphora shaped, and filled with a delicately colored *rosé*. This had come, so we were told, from the Ott vineyards in Bandol. It was subtle and it demanded attention, in a different world altogether from the rough-and-ready *rosé* we had tried in the past. As our friends said, "This is a real wine."

That was more than twenty years ago. Since then, the Ott influence has spread inland from the coast, and today there are dozens of vineyards throughout Provence that produce first-class *rosé*. Here in France, restaurant wine lists now have a separate *rosé* section. And this is not confined to Provence. America, Corsica, Australia, Italy, Spain, even England—they all have their own *rosé*. I still treasure the bottle of Great Wall Chinese *rosé* that we were given some years ago. The world seems to have gone pink, perhaps one small sign of an increasing desire for simplicity when we sit down to eat and drink.

Nine

❖❖❖

The Weather Is Here.
Wish You Were Beautiful.

*I*t is one of the few certainties in life: If you are fortunate enough to live in a lovely part of the world with a predictably excellent climate, guests will descend on you. Some will have been invited. Others will have invited themselves. They can be generous and entertaining, delighted with their surroundings, loudly appalled at the high prices they come across, keen to explore or content with a book by the pool, fascinated by the local inhabitants or irritated that they don't speak English, ready at a moment's notice to throw off their clothes and suck up the sun or to lurk in the shade and dodge the heat, amused by the Provençaux and their funny little ways or exasperated by those same funny little ways. In the course of many summers, we've seen them all.

The first signs of the guest season appear early in the year—often as early as January, when gray English weather, combined with the aftereffects of a surfeit of Christmas, make the thought of blue skies and sunshine irresistible. Our phone rings.

"Just thought I'd give you a call and see how you are. Surviving winter, I hope—it's bloody awful here." I look out of the window. The sky is, as usual, blue.

Now that the social niceties are over, the caller gets to the purpose of the call. "What are you up to this summer? Any plans for July?"

We don't have plans for July. We never do. It's too hot. We move slowly, eat the wonderful melons of the season for breakfast, enjoy long dinners outside in the cool of the evening, and stay at home. I pass this on.

"Oh, great. Because we're going to be driving down to the coast for a couple of weeks in July, and we'd love to drop by and say hello."

Experience has come to show us that "dropping by" is an elastic concept that can include as little as drinks and lunch or as much as a stay of several days. But back then we were still innocent in the ways of would-be guests. And the caller, if not exactly a close friend, is an acquaintance of some years' standing. It is agreed that he will call again when he has a date.

The months pass by, and that January call is forgotten. But then the phone rings again.

"Hi! We're just leaving Lyon. If the traffic's not too bad, we could be with you by lunchtime. Is that okay?"

I check with the long-suffering and infinitely kind-hearted Jennie, who nods her agreement. She has a more philosophical attitude toward guests than I do. She considers them a natural annual event, as much a part of summer as the heat. I once made the mistake of suggesting that you could say the same about mosquitoes. She didn't find that funny.

Shortly after one o'clock, the guests arrive, filled with horror stories about the perils of sharing the *autoroute* with lunatic French drivers. They have been on the road since getting off the cross-Channel ferry at the crack of dawn, and they are hot. And they are thirsty. Boy, are they thirsty. And they are anxious to make a few calls home (these being the distant days before cell phones). By the time they have attended to a bottle of *rosé* and their phone calls and taken a swim and a shower, it's almost four o'clock before we sit down to lunch.

Over coffee, we ask where they're going and where they're staying. The coast, they say, and they hope to find somewhere nice when they get there. They say they are "spur-of-the-moment" people.

You can guess the rest. We tell them that July is not the month for spurs of the moment. The coast is fully booked, and has been for months. Consternation sets in, and by now it's five thirty. Inevitably, it's agreed that they had better stay the night. One night stretches on to more nights. This, you might think, is an extreme example, but it has happened often enough to make us a little wary of spontaneous visits, although it's only fair to say that we've enjoyed most of them.

In complete contrast, there are the highly organized guests who like to *plan ahead*. They do their homework, and their calls usually begin several weeks before they're due to arrive, with detailed questions about the temperature, the program of local festivals, wardrobe hints, and the availability of remedies for upset stomachs. There are often thoughtful inquiries about what treats we would like them to bring over from England—tea, digestive biscuits, pork sausages, single-malt Scotch, a Harrods picnic hamper. These kind suggestions make us realize how thoroughly our tastes have changed after years of living in Provence, where a Harrods hamper is as rare as snow in August.

When our organized friends arrived, it was literally within minutes of when they said they would, and this punctuality set the tone for their stay. Their vacation was planned down to the last day, and on their first evening we heard all about it. A trip to Arles, to see a variety of marvels: the 100-foot-long Roman boat that was dredged up after spending two thousand years on the bed of the Rhône River, and which has been beautifully restored; a marble bust of Caesar, not surprisingly balding and wrinkled after his two thousand years underwater; the magnificent twenty-thousand-seat amphitheater, built in the year 90 as a setting for chariot races and gladiatorial contests, and now used for bullfights and concerts—the list went on and on.

After Arles, there was Cavaillon, for the *fête du melon*—banquets, parades, and the running of Camargue horses through the town with, *naturellement*, street-corner melon tastings. And, once the melon has settled down, a short evening drive over the Luberon to the Lourmarin music festival, a program of classical music, opera, and jazz, which runs all through the summer in the local fifteenth-century chateau.

This list, exhausting enough on its own, was far from complete. There were food festivals, wine festivals, the local weekly markets, the antiques colony and flea market at L'Isle-sur-la-Sorgue, and a healthy selection of restaurants. If our friends achieved half of what they had in mind, they were going to need a vacation afterward. Off they would go early each morning, returning home in the evening bursting with reports of what they had seen. They were, in many ways, ideal guests. They loved Provence. They entertained themselves, and later, with their descriptions of the day's discoveries, they entertained us. We look forward to having them back again.

It would be wrong to suggest that everyone has such a positive view of their time here. Critics and their criticisms have their moments, too, as can be seen from our list of the top ten guest gripes:

1. "It's so *hot*."
2. "Do the crickets always make so much noise at night? Or is it those damned frogs?"
3. "I think someone's put garlic in the marmalade."
4. "I can't get over how much people drink here. Do all the guys have beer for breakfast?"
5. "Why does everybody speak so fast?"
6. "The milk tastes funny."
7. "Why do those hunters have to start shooting so early on Sunday mornings?"
8. "Do they *have* to park their cars on the sidewalk?"
9. "Dogs in restaurants! Don't they know that's a health hazard?"
10. "It's so *hot*."

And yet, despite all this, these gluttons for punishment are planning to come back next year.

It usually takes only one visit during the high season to persuade our guests that their timing could perhaps be improved. Quite apart from the heat, July and August have suffered from years of overpopularity. These are the months when the French *en masse* are on vacation, and each year it seems that most of them have chosen the South of France. The crowds start in Paris and the north. They pile into their cars and converge on the southbound *autoroutes,* where multi-mile traffic jams and irate drivers are the rule rather than the exception. Eventually, they arrive, fractious, exhausted, and desperate for peace.

This is not always easy to find. Villages that for ten months a year are known for their sleepy charm have been transformed. The streets are jammed. People squabble over seats at café tables. Restaurants struggle to accommodate the midday rush, and the increased risk of being trodden on makes the village cats look for relief by crouching underneath parked cars.

For two-legged villagers, summer crowds can provide generous compensations. During these two hectic months, cafés, restaurants, and boutiques make their profits for the year. Landlords increase their rents. There is standing-room-only in the village pharmacy, with queues lining up in search of remedies for too much sun, too much food, and too much alcohol. The local artist sells his entire production of sketches and paintings in a couple of weeks. Wherever you look, business is booming.

Then comes the last weekend of August, and the sudden, almost instant change back to normality. The tourists have gone. The village breathes a sigh of relief, and sleepy charm returns. Villagers can once again stop to gossip in the main street without being run over by someone taking a selfie.

For us, September is the best month of the year. The temperature drops to a more comfortable level, although it's still warm enough to swim, and to eat outside in the evening. There's always a table free on the café terrace, or in our favorite restaurant. And Mother Nature, who has been busy all summer, is at her prolific best. The markets are overflowing with fruits and vegetables and lettuces that have been gathered early that morning. There are promising signs of activity in the vines. Normally, there will be a few welcome days of rain, to settle the dust and brighten up the green of the hillsides. In some ways, it feels like a second spring.

How lucky we are.

Ten

A Midsummer Night's Treat

For most of the week, it's nothing special, an old *coopérative fruitière*, where local producers used to sell what they had produced. A large area originally used for parking trucks and tractors, bordered by L-shape stone buildings, it's a good example of the kind of light-industrial architecture often found in rural parts of Provence—practical, no frills, and, until recently, no people. Now, thanks to a forward-looking mayor and some high-tech enthusiasts, it has become an IT center known as *La Fruitière Numérique*.

Each Tuesday evening between May and October, technology gives way to gastronomy in the form of a *marché nocturne*, an evening market with a difference. It has the great advantage of being just across the road from the center of Lourmarin, one of the prettiest and most popular villages in the Luberon. This in itself is enough to guarantee a good turnout.

Tourists and residents alike, having spent a tough day in the sun, can find shade and relief from the heat, enough wine to provide relief from thirst, a generous choice of fresh produce, and an introduction to some of the finer points of professional cuisine.

These are offered by a different local chef each week, often assisted by the mayor of Lourmarin, who acts as master of ceremonies, introducing the chef and his chosen subject. There are nine of these kitchen heroes, who take a break from their restaurants to demonstrate some of the tricks of their trade. One week it might be the secrets of a perfect pasta, made with local cherry tomatoes, local olives, and local olive oil. The next week could feature a sublime strawberry dessert. The menu is long, varied, fascinating, and simple. The audience, sitting on wooden benches, is rapt.

Before the turn of the chef, the market starts to become busy and, in high summer, the setting for an informal fashion show, featuring an abundance of cooked flesh. Among the ladies, shorts seem to get shorter and dresses more diaphanous every week, and the display of hats is enough to make a milliner swoon. Recently I saw, among the sea of Panamas, a vintage trilby, a couple of turbans, and what I imagine was an Australian sombrero, with one side of the brim pinned up in the style of a bush hat.

The dress code for men varies. At one end of the style spectrum, there is the occasional aging hippie, with gray ponytail (they've become increasingly popular), silver bracelets, and tattoos. At the other end are the Parisians with their sartorial guard down—suits replaced by well-pressed shorts, polo shirts, and suede moccasins, all spotless. They mingle in a swirl of relaxed humanity, with no visible pushing and shoving, and this *politesse* helps to create an unusually good-humored atmosphere. I have rarely seen such a well-behaved crowd, and they all seem to be enjoying themselves.

If you get to the market early enough, around six, you can not only choose your spot, but furnish it. Tin tables of various sizes have been placed well away from the food stalls, and there are plenty of folding chairs. But never quite enough, because there are always more bottoms than seats. With organized couples, this frequently leads to a division of responsibilities. The husband occupies the table, lays claim to two chairs, and guards the bottle of wine and two glasses while his wife goes short-distance shopping around the stalls, coming back to the table from time to time to have a quick sip and drop off provisions before returning to the stalls to carry on with her noble task.

She is spoiled for choice, but there are a couple of horrors she won't find. First, there is no trace of shrink wrap, bubble wrap, or any other form of plastic supermarket packaging: the growers like you to see what you're going to eat without any artificial trimmings. They are proud of what they've grown, whether it's fat white asparagus, fragrant peaches, or bouquets of chard. The sell-by date is this evening, just a few hours after the produce has been picked.

The second welcome absence is that dangerous vehicle, the supermarket cart. There is no risk of suffering a glancing blow or squashed feet after being run over by a cart whose pilot is too busy consulting her cell phone to look where she's going. The only shopping aid on wheels I've seen was what appeared to be an oversized, mechanized roller skate, driven by a German gentleman. The front and back wheels were joined by a short platform on which the driver stood. Steering was by a set of waist-high handlebars, and power came from a tiny noiseless engine. I watched as this ingenious contraption glided silently through the crowd and stopped at two or three stalls before returning to the driver's table with bulging shopping bags dangling from the handlebars. This was repeated several times, totally accident-free.

For those of us on foot, a tour of the stalls can take a very pleasant half hour, often more. Sausage lovers can find several varieties to nibble on. There are cheeses soft and hard, quiches large and small, and a selection of home-baked treats that varies from week to week. There are jams, and there are olive oils. The produce is displayed on tray upon tray, fruits and vegetables and herbs, all of it just picked; some, like the deep purple eggplant, are polished to a high level of gloss. Nothing contains preservatives, artificial colorings, or additives of any kind. In other words, nature has been left alone.

Browsing through the garlic is, as you can imagine, thirsty work, but the market organizers have come to the rescue: there's a bar. Small and simple it may be, but it is extremely well stocked with wine of all colors, on sale by the glass or, for advanced cases of dehydration, by the bottle. It was at the bar that we saw something I'm sure could only happen in France. A young girl, maybe nine years old, barely the height of the bar counter, waited patiently until her turn came. With impressive self-assurance, she ordered two glasses of Muscat, and slid a ten-euro note across to the barman, who brought her the wine. I assume that he thought she was just another customer, although shorter than most. At no time did he ask who the wine was for. I can't imagine this kind of nonchalance in an English pub or an American bar, where the very idea of an underage person getting anywhere near alcohol is cause for consternation and alarm. The barman, of

course, knew that the girl was being a good and duti-
ful daughter, taking the wine to her parents.

Around seven thirty, the market begins to look like
a sprawling self-service café. Most of the shopping
has been done, and it's time for further refreshment—
wine, of course, with a slice or two of cheese, sausage, or whatever else has just been bought from the
stalls. The mood is cheerful, the heat of the day has
given way to a pleasantly cool evening, and nobody
is in a rush to leave. Indeed, nobody is in a rush to
do anything except enjoy the moment, and it is often
nine thirty or so before the last customers are gone,
some of them having eaten everything they have just
bought. Never mind. There's always next Tuesday.

The whole evening has been a pleasure rather than
a chore. If there is a more civilized way to go food
shopping, I have yet to find it. And you will never need
a can opener to help you enjoy the food you've chosen.

Eleven

❖

Lunch Break

*L*unch is taken very seriously in Provence, as we quickly discovered. Local shops close between noon and two p.m. Business appointments, except those that include lunch, are rarely arranged if they conflict with the two sacred hours devoted to the stomach. There is a noticeable decrease in the amount of traffic on country roads, and the cafés fill up as the working day pauses for refreshment. A most civilized habit.

Weekend lunches are, if anything, even more strictly observed, particularly on Sundays, when the working-week two-hour break can easily extend to three hours or more. Very often, Sunday is a day when two or three generations of the family get together, and we have noticed how well behaved the young children are. It's not easy to sit quietly for three hours without a glass or two of wine, but there they are, good as gold, reading or, more likely, mesmerized by some electronic novelty.

As you will see from the short list below, we prefer simplicity to the complicated pomp that so many restaurants adopt in an effort to justify inflated bills. One sure sign of this is waiters in white gloves. Another giveaway is when the waiter murmurs in reverential tones describing what you have just ordered and what he has just put in front of you. This is inevitably accompanied by his pointing, with his cocked little finger, at the items on your plate. At one memorable dinner we were invited to in Paris by a couple of friends the ritual started with four waiters in attendance, each with a covered dish. These were placed with great ceremony in front of us, and all four covers were simultaneously removed with a flourish. Alas, there must have been a breakdown of communication in the kitchen, since we each found ourselves looking at food we hadn't ordered. We left shortly afterward.

There is no chance of this kind of culinary tragedy happening at any of our preferred restaurants. We've been going to them, often for several years, without finding a single white glove. What we have found is imaginative food served by friendly people in a relaxed atmosphere. What more could you want?

LA CLOSERIE, ANSOUIS

We became even more fond of this restaurant when it was awarded a Michelin star—and nothing changed. There were no frantic refurbishments, no huge price increases, and no ornamental dishes added to the menu; it stayed as it had always been, fresh, well balanced, and consistently good.

While food and service are excellent throughout the year, there are two seasons when Olivier, the chef, lets nature do an important part of the work. The first is spring, a time for asparagus in all its forms to make its annual appearance: with a dusting of Parmesan, roasted with garlic, drizzled with butter and balsamic vinegar or the classic *vinaigrette,* or a dozen other imaginative variations. These are best enjoyed outside, on the restaurant terrace, in the sunshine.

The second bonus from nature, the black truffle, comes at the end of the year, starting in November and going through until early February. This is the season when the crouched figures of truffle hunters and their dogs can often be seen in the woods around our house, trying to look as though they're just out for a stroll. I once made the mistake of asking one of these gentlemen if he had found any. At once, he became the picture of indignation. "Truffles?" he said.

"Moi? Jamais!" Even his dog did his best to look innocent. After all, truffles are among the most expensive mushrooms in the world, and it would never do to let amateurs like me know where they might be found. If you are ever fortunate enough to come across one, slice it up, put it in an omelette, and eat the evidence.

PERON, MARSEILLE

There are 1,837 restaurants in Marseille, but none with a more glorious view: the vast blue sweep of the Mediterranean and the four Frioul islands. The most famous of these is the Château d'If, once the prison where Edmond Dantès, the Count of Monte Cristo, spent several years before escaping disguised as a corpse (for the full story, read the book by Alexandre Dumas).

The view may be more famous than the menu, but the food comes a close second. Peron is known for its fish, although carnivores can always find their fillet of beef. But it would be a pity to miss the catch of the day, the prawns, the stuffed squid, and the many other delights provided by the neighboring sea. One dish above all gives you the traditional taste of Marseille, and that is Peron's specialty: the pedigree *bouillabaisse*.

This is perhaps the only dish on the menu that should carry a warning. You need to dress for it, and wear something that cleans up easily. *Bouillabaisse* is not something that can be eaten in neat bites. It is part soup, part fish stew; delicious, but difficult to control. Many an immaculate shirtfront has suffered from garlic-scented stains, and it is a wise customer who asks for two large napkins.

It all started several hundred years ago. Marseille's fishermen, coming back hungry after a hard day at sea, needed to eat. They put aside their most expensive fish to sell in the market, and instead found a way to use rockfish, shellfish, and fish that were more bone than flesh, and thus no good for restaurants. These were cooked in a cauldron, and seasoned with garlic and fennel. A contribution from America came in the seventeenth century in the form of tomatoes, until then unknown in Marseille.

Bouillabaisse made its slow but steady progress into restaurants and private kitchens, adding refinements along the way—olive oil, saffron, thyme, bay leaf, and onions—and, of course, the various fish. These are transformed into a broth and served with bread spread with a thick coating of *rouille,* a mayonnaise of olive oil, egg yolk, saffron, and crushed garlic cloves.

Those are the basics; there are many variations, all tasty and all messy. Keep a spare shirt handy.

LE COMPTOIR, LOURMARIN

Here is one of those pleasant surprises you sometimes find in Provence: a café with a chef. It is not unknown for customers to come for breakfast, linger through the morning watching the village come to life, and stay for lunch. There is a simple but varied menu that starts with open sandwiches and works its way up to the chef's specials of the day, which always include various forms of freshly made pasta.

Good as the pasta is, my own favorite dish is *bresaola*, and the way it is served. *Bresaola* is lean, top round beef that has been air-dried, salted, and left to age for two or three months until it is hard. It is then cut into thin, almost transparent slices. What happens to it after that at Le Comptoir is what makes it special. First, the sliced beef is laid out until it covers the plate. A little olive oil is added, followed by generous flakes of Parmesan. Tiny roasted potatoes are placed around the rim of the plate, a glass of good red wine is poured, and conversation comes to a halt as the first mouthful is taken and the taste buds spring to attention. For me, beef has never tasted so delicate.

But lunch is far from over. Some room must be left for a slice or two of *fiadone*, the Corsican version of cheesecake. The key ingredient is Corsica's favorite cheese, *brocciu*. This is mixed with milk, eggs, the zest of fresh lemons, and a nip of brandy. The taste will make you feel like hopping on a plane and going to Corsica for dinner.

LE NUMÉRO 9, LOURMARIN

Known simply as "Neuf" to its regular clients, this was a recent discovery—a small, charming room with a short, imaginative menu. If I were the restaurant's owner, I'd be tempted to keep the chef under lock and key; he's that good.

Neuf is run by two smiling ladies who have the priceless gift of providing smooth service without ever seeming to be rushed. You want to ask a question, change your mind about the wine, or reserve your dessert in advance (always a good idea)? Either Lyse or Patricia will be there. I suspect they have eyes in the back of their heads.

As for the food, I can't do better than invite you to share the menu we had on our last visit.

The meal started with *bouillabaisse*, but not the classical version that you find at Peron. This one was a perfect miniature, with all the complex flavor of its larger colleagues, but without the challenge of juggling the various elements. You could eat it with a soup spoon, and forget about feeling that you should take a shower afterward.

For the main course, the choice was between cab-
bage that had been stuffed with quail and decorated
with a slice of fresh *foie gras,* and tuna steak served on
a bed of zucchini and covered in the most delicious
sauce I've ever had. This was *condiment grenobloise,*
an inspired mixture of brown butter, capers, crou-
tons, parsley, and lemon. The thought of it makes my
mouth water.

But all was not yet over. We paid a visit to the
cheese board for something to help the last of the
wine go down, and then it was time for the traditional
ending to a lovely meal: *tarte fine aux pommes,* which
is apple tart taken to a celestial level. The apple, sliced
very fine, is arranged in a flat spiral on a thin base of
puff pastry and brushed with butter, honey, vanilla,
and Calvados. The result is a joy to look at and a memorable way to end what is always a memorable lunch.
Bravo, chef!

❦

One of the joys of traveling through Provence is finding yourself in the middle of one of the countless food
and wine festivals that start in the spring and carry
on through summer and fall. These are informal,
good-natured affairs, organized by people whose sole
desire is to give you a taste of pleasure, whether your

particular weakness is a fresh sardine or an elderly cheese. Naturally, they'd like you to buy something; to persuade you, they have developed the best of all sales techniques: a free trial. It is quite possible to have a junior version of a three-course lunch as you wander through the stalls—a slice of *saucisson* here, a slice of pizza there, a mouthful of goat cheese, a tempting fragment of apple tart, and, if you look thirsty, the odd glass of wine offered by the local *vignerons* who are waiting, corkscrews at the ready, for you to come along.

Most of the villages and towns in Provence have some kind of event to celebrate food and wine, even if it's only an extra few stalls in the weekly market. But, for the festival connoisseur, there are larger and more sophisticated celebrations. Here are just a few.

FÊTE DU RIZ, ARLES

Arles in the summer is one long festival: concerts, bullfighting, parades, and processions, even gladiator contests. And then, in the middle of September, three days are devoted to the glories of rice. The festivities start with the arrival of the "Ambassador of Rice," who has come up the Rhône by boat to open the proceedings. After that, it's rice in all its diversity, with plenty of music and entertainment.

FÊTE DES OLIVES VERTES, MOURIÈS

In the village of Mouriès, near Saint-Rémy, the young green olive has its annual moment of fame. The festival takes place during the second weekend in September, and it may be the only event in the world where you can watch a contest to decide who is the fastest olive crusher. And that's not all. As a change from olives you can watch a *cocarde,* in which bunches of rosettes are placed on a bull's horns, and the valiant *cocardiers*—young men dressed in white—try to remove the rosettes without being gored, perhaps by distracting the bull with a handful of crushed olives.

FÊTE DES TRUFFES, AUPS

Every year, on the fourth Sunday in January, a distinctive and expensive aroma permeates the village of Aups. This is a reminder that today is the annual truffle festival, when the normally secretive truffle hunter offers a glimpse of the tricks of his trade. There is a demonstration of the hunt—the sniffing, digging, and ultimate discovery—and a truffle dog competition, to find the most sensitive nose. There is, of course, a truffle market. And the village restaurants will all have truffles on the menu. An overdose of paradise for truffle lovers.

. . .

There are dozens of other festivals, of varying sizes and spectacles, and the passionate festival enthusiast can find something throughout most of the year. For instance:

MENTON, February/March—lemons in all
their glory

VENASQUE, early June—cherries

CAVAILLON, June/July—those wonderful
melons

PIOLENC, late August—garlic

RASTEAU, early November—chocolate and
wine

Almost anywhere, at almost any time—wine of all colors, signaled by roadside notices and posters

This brief selection supports the widely held conviction that, wherever you are in Provence, you need never go hungry.

Twelve

❖❖❖

Read All About It

*O*ne of the unexpected results of writing a well-received book is the sudden interest shown by journalists in the nonliterary aspects of your life. In my case, all kinds of things seem to interest them: what you eat for breakfast; whether or not you miss those dearly beloved aspects of English life like proper tea, the climate, and cricket; whether or not you still have English friends; and dozens of other matters that have nothing to do with books and writing. I once asked a journalist why he felt it necessary to bring these subjects up. "Readers love background," he said, nodding wisely.

"Now—about those dogs of yours. How long have you had them?"

During the past twenty-five years, I have sat through hundreds of interviews. Most of them took place on book tours, often on television, and what highly organized, precisely timed episodes they were, even if they did only last six minutes. Distinctly impersonal minutes they were, too, because as soon as the interviewer had asked his question and was no longer on camera, the host's attention would wander. He'd be making signals to his producer, looking at her signals to him, and, for all I knew, trying to decide where they should have lunch. I often felt that I was talking to myself.

Press interviews, of course, are very different, and it was a pleasant change to have people to talk to instead of a black camera lens. Journalists started to arrive in May and June, their numbers peaked in August, and they disappeared during the winter, just like vacationers. A couple of them indicated that I was not a serious journalistic subject, but a welcome relief from their normal assignments. As one of them put it, after a second glass of *rosé*, "If you had the choice between listening to a politician drone on about his agenda in some damp corner of Westminster or coming to sunny Provence for a few days, which one would you pick?" He was unusually frank, but I suspect he spoke for many of his colleagues.

The newspapers and magazines they worked for obviously influenced their questions. Journalists from what was often described as "the popular press" (ce-

lebrity gossip, football, pinups, and minimal news)
would ask if I had any famous readers, or if we had
any famous neighbors. At one point, they had heard
that Princess Diana had a property in Saint-Rémy-
de-Provence. Apart from her, in those days almost all
the well-known people with homes in Provence were
French. This usually provoked a slight curl of the lip,
and an evident drop in the attention level. When,
in answer to the next question, I had to admit that
I had never been to watch the local football team,
Olympique de Marseille, the interviewer could barely
hide his disappointment at failing to find a fruitful
subject to discuss. We were left with my most recent
book, which most journalists had been too busy to
read.

Next in line were the food journalists, who had
come, knife and fork at the ready, to comment on
the restaurants and all things edible that I had written about. It was a relief to find a subject of common
interest, and naturally, these interviews had to take
place over lunch, which made them pleasantly convivial. I enjoyed them, even when I was frog-marched
into the kitchen to pay our respects to the chef.

It was interesting to see the effects that these visits
by English journalists had on the chefs and owners of
the restaurants we went to. These were never sophis-

ticated establishments jockeying for another star in the *Guide Michelin,* but simple country restaurants where we were regular customers, and the chefs were clearly flattered and impressed that a journalist had come all the way from England to sample their cooking. To this day, I am likely to be offered a glass of *marc* on the house at the end of the meal by way of appreciation for the increase in British customers.

One unique experience was with the sports editor of a small suburban newspaper in Surrey, a prosperous area close to London. The sports he covered reflected the athletic preferences of his well-to-do, mostly middle-aged readers: golf (of course), tennis, and the venerable game of bowls, played on a tailored surface of immaculate deep green grass by stately ladies and gentlemen dressed in white. It's about as far from soccer as you can get.

The sports editor, who had come to the South of France to assess the golf courses, had been told that *boules,* a French version of bowls, was very popular in Provence. And so, sensing a sporting scoop for his paper, he had decided to leave the Riviera and come up to investigate. I told him what I could: the game had been invented in Provence, where it is called *pétanque* (derived from the Occitan dialect *petanca,* meaning feet fixed, or planted on the ground), and

I told him what I knew about the rules. That wasn't good enough; he wanted to see a match. We agreed to meet that evening at a nearby village where I suspected *boules* would be on offer.

An essential adjunct for any serious *boulodrome* location is the café, where exhausted players can refresh themselves, and where spectators can sit comfortably on the café terrace to watch the drama unfold. This is a tradition dating back to the early 1900s, and one that adds considerably to the game's popularity.

When we arrived, the journalist from Surrey was shocked to see the *terrain*, or the playing areas—rectangular courts of flattened earth or crushed stone. "They play on *that*?" he said, his voice a study in disbelief. "How can they gauge the run of the *boule*?" I was saved from having to answer by the start of the game in front of us, and he saw at once that it was a different kind of skill from the one required on smooth Surrey grass.

As the game continued, he became more and more interested. He admired the graceful throwing action of the players, the long, looping flight of their *boules*, and the ferocious accuracy with which they bombarded any of their competitors who had landed too close to the *cochonnet*. There was a lot to take in.

I saved the best until last by telling him the traditional way of marking a 13–0 result—the loser is expected to kiss the barmaid's bottom. "Good grief!" he said. "They'd never do that sort of thing in Surrey."

One other result of interviews that were published in the British press was that I began to receive letters from readers, and I've kept them all, hundreds of them. Most of them were to tell me how much they had enjoyed the book, which was kind. But a few readers, hot under the collar with indignation, wrote to tell me, without being specific, that I was ruining Provence. I wrote back, asking them how I was ruining it, but the only answer worth keeping was this one: "Your wretched book is in every lavatory in Wiltshire."

That particular comment was easy to laugh off, but there were a few other, less picturesque accusations that I tried to take seriously, only to find that they had often been made from positions of considerable ignorance. For instance, one critic whom I replied to admitted that he had only been to Provence twice in five years, for a total of ten days. Even so, he knew that it was being ruined because the price of a cup of coffee in his favorite café had just gone up by ten centimes.

Among all the correspondence from readers, there was only one truly unpleasant letter, from a man who told me that I wrote drivel. This was the least offensive of a string of insults which he ended by telling me that he had enclosed a twenty-franc banknote, because he was certain I would never make any money as a writer. The tone of the letter was enough to make me want to reply, and the writer had made the mistake of using stationery with his address on it. I'm afraid I couldn't resist. I sent his twenty-franc note back to him wrapped around a suppository. I never heard from him again.

My favorite letter came from a gentleman whose life, like mine, had undergone a drastic change. He was writing from his cell in Broadmoor, a well-known English prison, to tell me that reading a book of mine had given him, as he said, a day's reprieve from his sentence. He signed off with the reassuring words "Nothing serious. Out soon."

Letters were quite often replaced by personal visits. Readers who were on vacation would arrive at the house in cars, on bicycles, even on foot, looking for half an hour's distraction. In fact, it was sometimes a welcome distraction for me, too, a chance to leave the typewriter and my struggle with the alphabet, and sign a well-thumbed copy of a book or two. I'd go back to work greatly encouraged. There's nothing like an appreciative word from a satisfied reader.

One journalistic moment that I still treasure was

the interview conducted by a serious young man who came armed with questions I'd never been asked before. What was my father's occupation? Where had I gone to school? Did I have any children? I was puzzled by these questions because they had nothing to do with Provence, so I eventually asked the journalist where his interview was going to appear.

"Oh, didn't they tell you?" he said. "We're preparing your obituary."

Thirteen

A Good Place to Be Ill

There used to be a widespread belief among those Englishmen unfortunate enough to endure a privileged public school education that any health problem short of a broken leg could be cured by a couple of aspirin and a cold shower. Complaints and self-pity were for wimps, and a stoical disregard for aches, pains, and symptoms was admired.

This started to change several years ago, when girl students and their softening influence were admitted to these temples of learning, but for those of us who had been educated in the bad old days, old memories and insults remain. One insult in particular has stayed with me: it was always said that France is a nation of hypochondriacs. This was never explained or justified, probably because none of us had been to France or knew any French people, but it stuck, and it made us feel more manly and superior.

Early visits to France seemed to confirm that the French were considerably more health conscious than English schoolboys. There were more pharmacies, all equipped with chairs for those waiting their turn. And waiting time was often long, because each customer required a short conference rather than a quick purchase. Prescriptions were studied and discussed. One by one, packages of painkillers, digestive aids, trusses, eye drops, nose drops, and laxatives were arranged on the counter for consideration. Finally, when all the crucial decisions had been made, the customer would stagger out of the pharmacy with a bulging plastic sack containing enough to keep him healthy for at least another week.

This ritual was faithfully observed by the French, who were used to it. But for the poor ignorant foreigner, it was a little daunting. I still remember my first taste of pharmacy shopping. I had gone in to buy a tube of toothpaste. I found it, I took my place in one of the few chairs that was free, and I waited. And waited. And waited.

Eventually, my turn came, and I went up to the counter clutching my toothpaste. The pharmacist put it to one side, and asked to see my prescription.

"For toothpaste?"

"No, no. For your other purchases."

"I have no other purchases."

"*Ah, bon?*" His eyebrows went up in surprise. "*Bizarre.*" And he made a great ceremony of putting my toothpaste into a paper bag, folding the top carefully, sealing it with Scotch tape, and presenting it to me with a flourish.

My visit to the pharmacy made me curious about the French and their attitude to self-preservation, and I started to pay closer attention to what proved to be a rich and often surprising subject. For a start, I quickly learned the consequences of making polite inquiries about a Frenchman's general state of health: if you ask him how he is, he'll tell you, in detail, from his lower-back problems to his turbulent liver, his arthritic toe, and, if you're not careful, the irregularity of his bowel movements. This fascinating update will be delivered as if none of these conditions had ever been suffered before. Attempts to interrupt will be brushed aside, and all you can do is assume a sympathetic expression and hope that your companion will run out of ailments.

There is a story, widely told, about two elderly men having coffee one morning in the village.

"What are you doing today?" asked the first gentleman.

"Oh, I shall be at the doctor's most of this morning."

"Can I come?"

This exchange may well be true, such is the interest in medical matters. In doctors' waiting rooms, equipped with the usual varied selection of magazines, I've noticed that the most popular of these are journals devoted not to celebrities and soccer but to health problems. Waiting patients have their noses buried in news of the latest surgical advances, often tearing out a page that describes a breakthrough in the treatment of piles or heart fibrillation.

This fascination with our internal workings is not just personal. Other people's problems are every bit as interesting. When a friend of ours fell off his bicycle and broke a bone in his ankle, his plaster cast and his crutches made him a minor village celebrity, and the questions he was asked almost persuaded him to hand out a press release. It's only fair to say that the attention he received was entirely sympathetic. There was not even a trace of criticism that he often had a few beers before getting into the saddle, or his weakness for attacking the summit of Mont Ventoux after a good lunch. Instead, his questioners hoped that the problem wasn't too serious, and did he have any picturesque scars?

Scars are, of course, the most dramatic souvenirs of a brush with death, but they are by no means the only subjects of keen interest. Symptoms run them a close second, with the added advantage that we've all had symptoms at one time or another, and this allows us to join in the conversation.

Many years ago, I found myself sitting at a café table next to a group of old men whose behavior caught my eye. Instead of playing cards, they were having an animated discussion punctuated by frequent pauses: one man rolled up his shirtsleeves to allow a better view of his arms. The man next to him rolled up a leg of his pants. One by one, heads were massaged, necks were rubbed, and tongues extended. Then it was the turn of ribs and shoulders. In each case, the group paid close attention, asking questions, sometimes probing and poking the organ on display and generally acting as though they were having the most enthralling experience of their lives.

A week later, there they were again, the same old men, wearing their ailments like war wounds. After watching a second performance much like the first, I realized that this was a group dedicated to the appearance and progress of symptoms, the tracking of newly arrived aches, and the monitoring of degrees of suffering—all this helped down by health-giving carafes of *rosé*.

Sadly, when I went back to the café a few years later there was no sign of the symptomaniacs, and when I asked the café owner where they were, he shook his head, shrugged his shoulders, and drew his index finger across his throat. RIP.

Since then, I've seen smaller versions of this fascination with health, from two people arguing noisily over prescriptions to demonstrations of newly achieved mobility—the most public-spirited example being a friend of mine, who donated his recently discarded crutch to the café as emergency aid to customers who had enjoyed themselves slightly too much at the bar. In every case, what struck me was the willingness to share intimate personal health developments with the rest of the world.

My own experience with the French public health system has, on the whole, been pretty good. Our doctor, Madame Medicine, is charming and helpful, and writes embarrassingly generous prescriptions. Specialists are highly qualified and well organized. Pharmacists are extremely well trained and well informed. France must be one of the best places in the world to find professional medical help. And this occasionally comes with some surprising refinements, one of which I experienced not long ago.

Madame Medicine had suggested, then recommended, then insisted that I should undergo a minor operation. "Your heart is murmuring," she said, "and it's telling you to go to the hospital. Fortunately, I know an excellent man for hearts." And within forty-eight hours she called to give me my marching orders.

After the obligatory mechanical checks at the hospital, I was taken to see the surgeon, a reassuringly soothing young man who asked me if I had any sinful habits, like nicotine or cocaine. I was able to put his mind at rest about those, but I had to admit a long-standing fondness for red, white, and pink wines. He brushed those aside. *"C'est normal,"* he said. Obviously, a doctor after my own heart.

The great day arrived, and I was taken to my room at the hospital, where I found the doctor waiting to greet me. He told me that I needed to have a small preparatory procedure before the main event, and that he'd see me in the operating theater. I was then left to change into my outfit for the morning.

I don't know who invented hospital gowns, but it would be difficult to imagine a more embarrassing garment. Its flimsy cotton had a slit from neck to hem of what I assumed was the back of the gown. I put it on, and immediately discovered that, with any kind of movement, the slit fell open to reveal a detailed view of naked back and naked buttocks. I was still trying to work out some way of getting to the operating theater while preserving a shred of dignity when there was a knock on the door.

It was a girl, a pretty girl, carrying a small metal

tray. *"Il faut raser la barbe,"* she said with a grin. This puzzled me, as I've never had a beard. The girl then put her tray on the bedside table and I could see an electric razor, a cloth, and a small pot of what I imagined was after-shave balm.

"Lie down on your back, please," she said. I lay down. With great delicacy and precision she pulled the gown up to my waist, and I belatedly realized that I was about to have my very first pubic shave.

"Uncross your legs, please, and relax."

She gently went to work, and I have to say I didn't feel a thing. She finished, sat back, and surveyed her work.

"Voilà," she said with another grin as she dusted me off. "You look ten years younger."

Fourteen

The Pulse of the Village

The hours are brutal. You start as early as six a.m. and very rarely finish before ten p.m. During that long day, you will be expected to provide a variety of refreshments, operate as an occasional left-luggage facility, serve as an informal message center, and, most important of all, demonstrate endless patience and a receptive ear. In other words, you will be running a village café.

The café is much more than just a place to get a quick cup of coffee or a drink. In fact, it's a most useful and civilized compromise. More comfortable than perching on a barstool, less formal than sitting at a restaurant table, it is also a most welcoming destination for customers who, for one reason or another, are on their own. Sitting by yourself in a restaurant goes against human nature; man does not live by eating alone. But sitting by yourself in a busy café, you will usually find yourself in the company of several others who, for various reasons, prefer the companionable solitude offered by a table for one.

Not far from your seat on the terrace will be a man who is a human fixture at almost every French village café. This is the regular with his newspaper, sitting at his regular table at the back of the terrace, where he can see everyone. He doesn't need to order, because he has the same thing every morning. He will acknowledge people he knows with a nod before returning to his newspaper. He could be there for half an hour, or most of the morning. At no time will he be pestered into ordering something from the café bar; this too is preordained. If he is still at his table at eleven o'clock, a *pastis* and a small saucer of olives will be brought to him.

That is by no means all that will be brought to him in the course of the morning. Despite his relaxed, almost drowsy appearance, the regular is keen to know what's going on, to hear the day's nuggets of gossip. In one case I have in mind, these are supplied by Laure, a local café owner, who will have picked up the early-morning news from her privileged position behind the bar. She will come out for a quick session with the regulars to pass on items of particular interest: the latest developments in a village feud; rumors of the postman's sizzling new romance; a power struggle in the *mairie;* the chef's dog giving birth to half a dozen puppies in the kitchen of his restaurant—every day there is something new, and there is no better way to hear about it than from Laure, the village's very own CNN. Meanwhile, unaware of all this excitement, the group of tourists at the next table will be congratulating themselves on having found this marvelously peaceful village where nothing happens.

The peace is disturbed by a variety of new arrivals, none more colorful than a group of refugees from their very own *tour de France,* cyclists in desperate need of cold beer before they attack the next hill. They are, to a man, dressed like professionals, with lightweight crash helmets, bright yellow jerseys, and skintight black shorts. There is much clattering while they park their streamlined bicycles before mopping their heated brows and sinking their first beer so fast that the waitress is barely back inside the café before they call her out again for another.

By now, the terrace is becoming busier with what a local wag likes to call the summer League of Nations: British, Germans, and Dutch escaping from the gray chill of the northern summer; Parisians seeing how the southern half lives; and, in recent years, orderly groups of Japanese and Chinese. These latter visitors can be seen drifting down the main street of the village in docile pairs, talking quietly—so quietly, in fact, that it prompts some café regulars to wonder whether noisy people actually exist on the other side of the world.

And so the ebb and flow of village life continues throughout the morning until the street suddenly becomes less crowded and the café tables overflow with lunchtime diners. The level of chatter rises, and the waitresses perform miracles of balance as they wriggle among the tables, their trays loaded with bottles, glasses, platefuls of the *plat du jour,* and whatever can be cooked on the indoor barbecue. A favorite dish is *figatelli,* the rich and wonderfully tasty Corsican pork sausage, served with a large baked potato and guaranteed to get you through the afternoon.

By about three, the café terrace is once again sleepy and sparsely populated. Some customers have gone to answer the call of the siesta; others are up to their necks in the cool water of their pool. The café waitresses breathe a sigh of relief, and Laure, finally, can have a late lunch.

But quiet though the afternoon may be, it is often the preferred time for some highly personal activity as Laure becomes a one-woman advice center for those with problems. These will vary enormously: a dispute with the neighbors; an ill-advised affair; a grasping bank manager; a doctor who doesn't seem to care; a son with adolescent traumas; a daughter struggling with early womanhood; and, inevitably, those minor ailments that the French take such pleasure in discussing. All of these are listened to intently, and Laure's opinion is given when asked for. But advice is by no means the only part of the service offered. By far the most appreciated benefit of these consultations is that they provide a sympathetic audience and a measure of comfort for those who are going through difficulties. It's not all that different from a visit to a psychiatrist, except that you're more likely to get a glass of wine than a bill.

In Provence, there is a dramatic difference between the sweltering, hectic days of summer and the quiet, icy, almost deserted weeks of winter. This is the annual problem faced by the café's personnel director, who is, once again, Laure. In the winter, she can count on her husband to lend a hand when he's not pruning in the vineyard, and she has Annie, her permanent treasure, a local girl who has worked at the café since she was a teenager some years ago. But in the summer, this is not enough. Four or five more are needed to cope with the crowds.

Luckily, there are always plenty of students on vacation looking for some pocket money, and in the high season it is not unknown for your coffee to be served to you by a young woman on the brink of a degree in applied physics. But as willing as these summer recruits are, they have a lot to learn about essential café procedures. This is where Annie is invaluable, and this is when part of the terrace turns into her classroom, where she can pass on what she has learned over the years of active café duty. She runs a tight class, helped by a sharp eye for detail and the disposition of a sergeant-major.

Her summer day has started with an inspection of her part-time team. Are their fingernails and clothes clean? Are any explicit tattoos covered up? And while a little cleavage is good for business, some modesty must be observed. With these basics checked out, the morning's work can begin. And here, Annie's eye misses nothing. If a table has been left uncleared for too long, the delinquent waitress will be notified by a jerk of the head to indicate the problem, and a nod to encourage its fast solution. If a passing village dog has chosen to irrigate the leg of an unoccupied chair, Annie will order the prompt delivery of mop and bucket. If an absentminded customer has just left without taking her shopping bag, the most fleet-footed waitress will be delegated to run after her and return the bag. There is always something to be done to ensure that the dozens of customers who pass through every day have had a pleasant few moments in the café, and Annie is there to make sure that everything is done correctly, nipping at the heels of her waitresses like a sheepdog with an unruly flock.

Elsewhere in France, it is a sad fact that the number of cafés has been dwindling as the fast-food industry expands and as habits have changed. There is a distinct danger, for example, that the cell phone will one day replace face-to-face conversation, and that the *figatelli* will give way to the monsterburger. But for the moment, the traditional café is safe, at least in Provence, and, I imagine, in other parts of rural France. Long may that continue. It would be a tragic loss if this unique and delightful institution were to go the way of so many other victims of modern life.

Fifteen

---❖---

Snapshots

$\mathcal{M}$y wife, Jennie, is an indefatigable photographer, with a good eye for a quirky subject, and during the years we have lived in Provence she has filled everything from shoe boxes to industrial-sized cartons with her photographs. You can see a very small selection in these pages—unposed and unretouched, often taken on the run and, as she herself says, never going to compete with the highly polished efforts of the professional photographer. They are instead her informal record of moments and memories, and a glimpse of daily life in rural Provence. I hope she never stops.

OUR NEIGHBORS

Here we have an advance guard of the *sangliers,* or wild boar, that live in the forest above the house. In summer, they come down looking for water, and they have discovered that we have a pool. It hasn't happened yet, but it's only a matter of time before we find one of them taking his ease in the shallow end.

This would be a well-deserved consolation in his otherwise difficult life.

In the summer, he has to walk miles to get a drink; in winter, he has to be constantly on the lookout for hunters, with their dogs and their guns. Despite this, the *sanglier* doesn't seem to harbor any ill will toward humans, preferring to avoid them rather than make a nuisance of himself, which is more than one can say about some neighbors.

THE GARLIC BOUTIQUE

In Provence, it is not enough merely to cultivate great things to eat. They must be displayed in a way that does them justice. And garlic, which my friend Monsieur Farigoule describes as "one of nature's jewels"—or, if he's in a less poetic mood, "the stinking rose"—is a fine example of edible art.

What you see here are heads of garlic. Inside each head are the cloves that are used for cooking. Depending on the type of garlic, there can be anything from half a dozen cloves to thirty or more per head. Intense and powerful, they are known for their pungent and long-lasting effect on the breath. What is perhaps not as well known is that garlic is extremely good for you, with vitamin C, vitamin B₁, Vitamin B₆, calcium, iron, and potassium among the elements that keep a body healthy. In the hands of a good cook, it makes food taste delicious. And it is claimed to add a certain *je ne sais quoi* to the male sex drive. Not bad for a stinking rose.

A FIELD OF FLOWERS, PROVENCE STYLE

One of the joys of traveling along the back roads of Provence is the extravagant show that nature puts on for most of the year. Even in deep winter, the orderly rows of naked vines that seem to stretch for miles promise a greener, more luxuriant future. When spring comes, fields that have been flat and empty are, almost overnight, it seems, under a carpet of growth, with young leaves and shoots, and crimson splashes of poppies. And the drab winter clumps of lavender begin to show traces of the glorious color that blooms in high summer.

But nothing compares with the spectacular, almost shocking arrival of the sunflowers, acre upon acre of brilliant yellow, a sight that made van Gogh reach instantly for his brush. However, there's more to a sunflower than just a pretty face. Some years ago, I was told by Jerome, a wise old peasant, that he could tell me the approximate time of day by looking at a field of sunflowers. Their heads, which face east in the early morning, turn in the course of the day to follow the sun as it travels west. This is called solar tracking. Or phototropism. Or, as Jerome puts it, *un miracle.*

THE SMALLEST GUEST

This photograph marks a turning point in the gastronomic habits of the red-breasted robin—the morning he gave up his customary breakfast of worms for the delights of Jennie's cornflakes.

DIGGING FOR GOLD

When truffle hunters get together, the conversation often turns to the eternal question: Who makes a better sniffer—the pig or the dog? Supporters of the pig are convinced that the porcine snout is superior to the canine nose when it comes to detecting truffles, able to pick up that distinctive scent from far, far away. Nonsense, says the dog lobby. A good hound, properly trained, can outsniff a pig every time.

Our friend Regis, whom you see here hard at work,

is convinced that his dog Flip has the most successful nose in Provence, capable of earning a small fortune each winter. In 2016, good truffles were selling for $1,200 per pound, and so dogs like Flip, who can make a few thousand dollars during the season, are highly prized. Regis has even thought of putting Flip out to stud in the summer, but decided against it, thinking romance might go to his head and confuse his sense of smell.

ESSENTIAL EQUIPMENT FOR GRAPE PICKERS

This is perhaps the most picturesque item of agricultural equipment in the Provençal farmer's arsenal. Examples of the parasol start to appear early in September, when the vineyards are beginning to deliver what they have been growing all summer—ripe grapes, ready for the bottle. Picking them is hot, slow work, and attempts have been made to use machines instead of people. But, as with so much in Provence, old habits die hard. When it comes to your precious grapes, you trust the people you know rather than a complicated piece of machinery. This is why friends and members of the family are often promoted to the important post of grape picker, forming small groups scattered among the vines.

Although separated by distance, the pickers see no reason not to speak to one another, and their loud, cheerful conversations lend a convivial air to the vineyard. Lunch is taken in the shade of one of the parasols, and what could have been a boring chore is transformed into a pleasurable, sociable day. Who needs mechanical grape pickers?

ON YOUR MARK, GET SET . . . GOAT!

August 15, in Bonnieux, is a great day in the sporting calendar of the village, a day when normally peaceful streets become the setting for a duel between ten highly competitive contestants: the goat race, sponsored by the Café César.

As far as I know, this is a unique event. The goat, after all, is known more for his bizarre eating habits than for his speed on the racetrack. But these goats are different. Each of them has a coach, or driver. These specialists have trained their goats over the long months preceding the event, feeding them like champions, trying to teach them the skills of overtaking and cornering at speed, and generally ensuring their match fitness.

The race is scheduled to start at ten o'clock, and we arrive early, to find the village already in a high state of excitement. The ten drivers, burly men for the most part, are calming their pre-race nerves with beer. Their goats, busy nibbling at the café flower bed, are seemingly unconcerned that their athletic prowess is about to face a brutal test.

The start is slightly delayed so that the goats who are still nibbling can be turned to face the right way, and then they are off, their drivers running by their side to provide verbal encouragement and the odd helpful shove.

As we make our way up to the finish line, we can hear the cheers of the crowd mixed with laughter. The winning driver comes into view, panting, sweating, red-faced, and furious. Somehow or other, his goat has given him the slip.

SNOW? IN PROVENCE?

It happens. Not often enough to rate an annual snowfall statistic, but it certainly happens. And when it does, it gives us some of the most beautiful days of the year. If the snow has fallen overnight, the mornings are magical, with bright sunshine and dense blue skies. The countryside is dazzling white and unnaturally silent. After the dogs' morning walk in the forest, their whiskers are stiff with snow. Trees and bushes look as though they have been carefully decorated,

Our neighbors

❖

The garlic boutique

A field of flowers, Provence style

❧⸻❧

A beautiful workplace

The smallest guest

---◆❀◆---

Digging for gold

*Essential equipment
for grape pickers*

*On your mark, get set . . .
goat!*

—❀—

Snow? In Provence?

One for the road

❖

Advanced gardening

The first of the year

❖

Ah, spring!

Picturesque shopping

Another unexpected guest

✦

An extremely large back garden

and the heron who comes to paddle in our pond looking for breakfast is clearly puzzled to find that the surface is now a sheet of ice.

Down in the village, the snow has brought out seldom-used and often vintage articles of clothing: Grandpapa's fur hat; an ex-army greatcoat that dates back to the First World War; boots, stiffened by time, that creak with unaccustomed exercise—anything that keeps out the cold, and to hell with fashion.

The chilly temperature will often turn warm overnight, and we will wake up to find the snow gone. But for the moment, it's like living in a Christmas card.

ONE FOR THE ROAD

Village markets in Provence are usually restricted to one day a week. What is here today, bustling and crowded, is gone tomorrow, to become once again the half-empty village parking lot. This creates a serious problem for the thirsty marketeer, since village parking lots rarely have bars.

He need suffer no more, thanks to the mobile wine bar, provided by the Cave Vinicole du Luberon, which serves many of the local markets. Convenient, and fully stocked with red, white, and *rosé*, it is always well attended. Wives park their husbands there while they do their shopping. This frequently leads to husbands breaking the habit of a lifetime by volunteering to come and share the weekly market chore, in a supervisory capacity, of course, where they might well run into other equally considerate and thirsty husbands.

ADVANCED GARDENING

Every spring, some fields that have lain idle during the winter are transformed into future vineyards, and I am always impressed by the perfectly straight, perfectly spaced lines of young vines that are planted by the farmer and his tractor. How is it, I wonder, that the tractor driver, often with his back to what he's planting, can achieve this kind of immaculate symmetry? Does he have some kind of sophisticated device fitted to the tractor?

Not exactly. In fact, he has something better: his wife, she who must be obeyed as she walks a few paces behind or in front of him offering adjustments and instructions. It's a wonderfully simple and effective system, and it seems that there is no shortage in Provence of wives who are gifted with the all-seeing eye that helps to place the vines exactly where they should be, and where they will be for decades to come. *Bravo les femmes!*

THE FIRST OF THE YEAR

In Provence, you can eat according to the seasons, rather than what the supermarket has dug out of the deep freeze, and perhaps the best season is May and June. At this time of year, the fresh-food addict is spoiled for choice, with new garlic, broad beans, chives, spring peas, and strawberries on the market menu. But for most of us, the season really begins with the arrival of what Monsieur Farigoule calls "that noble weed," otherwise known as asparagus.

Everyone seems to have a favorite way of preparing this supremely versatile vegetable. It can be baked, roasted, pickled, or fried; used in risottos and countless different salads; chopped, shaved, and puréed.

Or, you can do what we prefer to do, and keep it simple: drizzle the asparagus with olive oil, add a little grated Parmesan, and pour yourself a glass of *rosé*. Heaven.

PICTURESQUE SHOPPING

The supermarket is a wonderful invention—efficient, convenient, virtually unlimited choice, and everything squeaky-plastic clean. But even its most ardent fans would admit that it has precious little charm.

Here you see a delightful alternative: the weekly

market in the village of Cucuron, where the stalls are set out around the shimmering rectangle of one of the biggest *bassins* in Provence. It's true that you won't find here several of the essentials of modern life. This isn't the place to come for canned and deep-frozen products, dishwashing liquid, pre-packed dinners for two, or deodorant.

But if your shopping list includes fresh fruits, fresh vegetables, local cheeses, the odd curious kitchen gadget, a variety of sausages, ham on the bone, and wine from the village *marchand de vins*, you won't be disappointed. And even if you buy nothing except a cup of coffee in the market café, you will have spent the morning in lyrical surroundings you won't forget for a long time.

AH, SPRING!

Winter has ended, with January just a chilly memory. Little by little, the days become longer and lighter. And then, sometime toward the end of March, spring arrives, seemingly overnight. Trees that had been gray and skeletal are suddenly smothered in blossom. The sun is hotter.

In the undergrowth, nature's orchestra, led by the frogs, begins tuning up for its summer performance. It's still too early for the stars of the show, the *cigales*, but even without them the sound is evocative, promising long, warm evenings spent outside.

The village becomes busier. Café regulars, who have spent winter hibernating inside, are now installed outside on the terrace. The markets are overflowing with spring treats—fruits and vegetables in dazzling abundance, and the hero of the moment, spring asparagus, the noble weed itself, is carefully laid out in tempting rows.

Spring is a wonderful season; not too hot, not too crowded, with the prospect of four or five months of sunshine to come. And asparagus for dinner.

ANOTHER UNEXPECTED GUEST

There she was one morning, standing on the roof enjoying the view, a classic specimen of the Provençal hunting dog. She didn't seem at all surprised to see us, but was clearly interested in our two dogs, and made her precarious way down from the roof to say *bonjour*. She was to be part of our lives for several weeks.

We lured her inside, where it soon became obvious that she had never been in a house. But she quickly worked out that the best place to be was the kitchen, where all kinds of good things were almost within reach, and she learned to hover optimistically at Jennie's feet.

In many ways she was like a docile wild animal, and it wasn't until the early evening that the wild instinct took over and she disappeared into the forest, where she would spend the night, only to be back on the roof in the morning, ready for breakfast.

We tried to find out where she had come from, but she had neither a collar nor a tattoo, and none of the local hunters came looking for her. And so it began to seem that we now had three dogs, even if one of them was only part-time.

Sadly, instinct was stronger than the comforts of domesticity, and she couldn't resist the forest. We haven't seen her now for months. But we still check the roof every morning, just in case.

AN EXTREMELY LARGE BACK GARDEN

Provence has more than its fair share of beautifully barbered and manicured formal gardens. These fine examples of neatness and order, in which even the leaves and twigs appear to have been precisely placed, are greatly admired. Lifestyle magazines feature them. Proud owners open them to the public for scheduled visits, and they are generally considered to be among gardening's major achievements.

However, they have an irresistible competitor, proving once again that man cannot win against nature. Throughout Provence, sometimes in the most unlikely spots, you will come across magnificent displays that have not been planted, watered, arranged, or primped into perfection. This huge field of poppies is a spectacular example. All too soon, the poppies will be gone. But they'll be back, to remind us of what nature can do if she's left alone to do it.

Sixteen

❖

The Weather Forecast: More to Come

The English in Provence are generally well received, even though they speak a curious, illogical language and have a dangerous tendency to drive on the wrong side of the road. But these are minor oddities when compared with their obsession with the weather, their deep distrust of meteorological predictions, and their conviction that if it isn't raining today, it will certainly come down in buckets tomorrow. This climatic distrust is reflected in their holiday habits, and it is the cause of great amusement among the Provençaux.

There is plenty to amuse them. For example:

On a rare gray day, when the atmosphere in the village is noticeably subdued, the Englishman can be heard encouraging the villagers in the café to cheer up with a phrase that is used to take the sting out of all kinds of calamities, from a drop in the value of the euro to an outbreak of swine fever in the Luberon. "At least it isn't raining," he will say to his bemused audience, with a jolly smile and an apparently genuine belief that this will make all well with the world.

In August, on a crowded beach reserved for serious nudists, there is one sure way of identifying the Englishman: he is the only sunbather to have brought along his trusty black umbrella. When this attracts attention, and a few incredulous questions, he will look up at the cloudless sky, shake his head, and say, "Well, you never know—very changeable thing, the weather."

Seen in a purely historical context, you can understand his caution. Having spent his adult life in England, a country where the climate allows you to experience three, and occasionally four, seasons in the same day, he knows that you can't count on a sunny morning turning into a sunny afternoon, and he needs to be prepared. In extreme cases, he will also have brought to the beach his carefully folded plastic raincoat.

Each spring, from April onward, the English *en vacances* display a more carefree attitude to the weather than our friend on the beach with his umbrella, an attitude that inspires puzzled discussions in the café: What is the crucial temperature that makes the English discard their clothing? When the rest of the village is still in sweaters, full-length pants, and the essential scarves, we see our English visitors dressed for high summer in their shorts and T-shirts and summer-weight dresses, apparently oblivious to the chill in the air that threatens to turn their bare knees blue.

This is merely a preview of what is to come: a habit that I have heard described as *le masochisme anglais*—the pre-lunch plunge into the pool, an almost obligatory ritual to greet the arrival of spring, and to hell with the brisk temperature. We are, after all, in Provence, which is well known for having, by English standards, an almost subtropical climate. I have often thought that it would take sheet ice to keep a determined Englishman from taking his first dip of the year.

But the Provençaux themselves are not without some quirks when it comes to dealing with the weather. When the sun doesn't shine and the light turns from bright and clear to dull and gray, they become morose, casting accusing glances at the sky and grumbling about this unreliable weather that threatens Provençal agriculture. Strangely enough, this is often improved if an Englishman should come into view, which provides the opportunity to deliver what might be Provence's all-time favorite weather cliché.

Let's say you've met Jean-Jacques, an acquaintance, in the street. It is one of those gray mornings, and this is reflected in his appearance. He looks ill-tempered and glum, his ruddy, normally cheerful face set in an expression usually reserved for discussing politics. In reply to your inquiries about his general state of health, he shakes his head, looks upward at the sky, and shrugs. As if activated by a signal, it starts to rain. Jean-Jacques's expression changes, and a glint appears in his eye as he nods upward again at the gathering clouds. *"Merde,"* he says, with obvious relish, *"eh oui—c'est comme un beau jour au mois d'aout en Angleterre."* I must have heard this dozens of times, often accompanied by a poke in the ribs to make sure I was paying attention and ready to laugh. Eventually, I started asking the weather experts if they had ever been to England, to experience at first hand that mythical fine day in August, only to find that most of them had never left Provence.

Every season has its experts, none more ready to alarm you than the motorist, as the brief but often icy winter begins. Throughout the year, the driving population of Provence is divided between tortoises and hares, and freezing weather accentuates the difference between them. The tortoises will bring out the old horror stories of ten-car pile-ups caused by patches of black (and therefore almost invisible) ice.

The solution: slow down. But the would-be Formula One driver will actually tell you that speed is safer, that the added danger of an ice-slicked road improves his reactions, his judgment, and his timing, not to mention the macho thrill of overtaking those elderly ladies dawdling along at fifty kilometers an hour. Not surprisingly, he has his enemies, led by the army of truck drivers who do their best to deliver in any weather, despite anything that nature throws at them. Unlike elderly ladies, they refuse to cower in the verge to allow a little extra room for passing. Often the opposite. When they hear the insistent blare of a horn behind them, they increase speed, and edge over until they occupy more road space. War is declared. The blarings continue, each one from behind echoed by an answering fusillade from the truck, until the stage is set for the final act.

The problem here is that the Frenchman's fondness for the physical gesture is hindered by the demands of steering, which limits the use of both hands. However, all is not lost. At last, the road widens, the pursuing car begins to draw level, and the driver lowers his window so that, as he finally passes the truck, he can stretch out one arm, the rigid second finger of his hand extended, to present the truck driver with the classic insult before accelerating away.

Less dangerous and more elegant was the response

of Michel, a friend of ours who enjoys taking his pony and trap and sometimes me for a spin on the narrow country road between his house and the village post office. The road is always quiet, often empty, and a large sign at its entrance forbids trucks. Even so, we had barely set off for the village one morning before we heard a muffled clatter, and then a shuddering mechanical wheeze behind us. I looked around, and there was a vast, multiwheeled truck, almost as wide as the road itself. Michel was unconcerned. "It doesn't happen often. The driver will have to be patient."

He may have tried, but he couldn't resist a couple of optimistic toots on his horn. In reply, Michel raised his whip above his head and twirled it several times. Was this a message of defiance, I wondered, or merely an acknowledgment? I asked Michel if it had a special meaning. "I'm sure it does," he said, "but I've forgotten. I'm turning left, I'm turning right, I'm lost—I think it's one of those."

Whatever it meant, it was enough to keep the truck driver more or less silent until we reached the end of the road and the start of something with two lanes. Michel pulled onto the shoulder, stopped, and climbed down from his seat. He took off his ancient brown hat, and with a bow and a flourish used it to direct the truck onto the larger road. It was the first and only time I have seen a truck driver smile.

. . .

No matter what season it is, Provence is never free from the possibility of attack by the ultimate weather quirk, the larger-than-life *mistral*. Once, during our early days in Provence, I made the mistake of saying to Faustin, our neighbor, what a windy day it was.

Clinging to his hat with one hand, he set me straight. No, no, no, he said, this is the *mistral*, powerful enough to blow old ladies across the street, and to uproot the ears from a donkey. What would be called fierce winds where you come from, he said, are no more than breezes to us. He spoke of it with a hint of pride, as though the *mistral* belonged to him, and I was to find that in Provence it is often regarded as though it were a minor national treasure rather than a violent hiccup in the weather.

More than almost anything else, the *mistral* is a wonderfully versatile excuse. I have heard it used to explain not only displaced roof tiles, but also headaches, dogfights, missed appointments, lumbago, marital squabbles, temperamental cement mixers, road accidents, and collapsed soufflés. Its unarguable strength is that it's nobody's fault, and so nobody can be blamed. And it doesn't confine itself to a particular season. Even in high summer it howls, usually for periods of three, six, or nine days.

It would be remiss, in any study of the weather, however informal, if there weren't a few statistics to make everything official. And here they are, starting with the one that surprised me most.

London, that famously moist and drizzly city, has an annual rainfall of 23.4 inches. The annual average in Cannes, where bikinis outnumber raincoats, is more than 30 inches, and, at 28 inches per year, the rainfall in Gordes is still considerably more than in London. These are just two examples of reality failing to live up to reputation. In an attempt to even things out, I searched for somewhere, anywhere in the UK, that offered the three hundred days or more of sunshine each year enjoyed by dozens of towns, villages, and beaches in Provence. No luck.

So *bonnes vacances,* and if you're going to Cannes, don't forget your umbrella.

Seventeen

◆❖◆

Blind Luck

*I*n the long and shaggy history of man's relation-ship with dogs, one event stands out as a funda-mental moment of change: the decision to give the dog shelter and let him become closely involved in human life. No longer obliged to spend his days out-side as a burglar alarm with teeth, he soon began to take advantage of his greatly improved career choices. From very early days, he became proficient at work-ing with man to herd sheep, cattle, goats, and horses. This led to a variety of activities developed over the centuries, and today we see dogs using their noses to find everything from black truffles to drugs, the bodies of people buried in rubble after an accident, bombs, and personal items lost down the back of the family sofa. There has also been an increase in the number of dogs recruited for police work, and no army regiment worth the name is without its highly decorated four-legged regimental mascot.

Surprisingly, it took until 1916 before a dog's talents were officially put to work to help the blind. It was then that the world's first guide dog school opened in Germany and quickly inspired a network of schools throughout the country. Eventually, other countries followed, and guide dogs became available for lucky adults. In those early days, blind children had to wait until they were eighteen, because anyone younger was considered "insufficiently mature."

And then came MIRA, a nonprofit organization based in Quebec. It started with two dogs in 1981, and by 1991 was well enough established to open the world's first school for blind children and their dogs.

Thousands of miles away, in Provence, news of MIRA's school reached Frédéric Gaillane, a man who was, in one way, uniquely qualified to become involved in the project himself. He had lost his sight in a car accident when he was nineteen, and he was only too familiar with the struggle of forging a very different life. And so, in 2004, he went to Canada to meet the founder of MIRA, Eric St. Pierre.

The two men got on well. Frédéric was impressed with what he found, and he returned to Provence filled with enthusiasm and ideas. He would, he decided, start a school for blind children. In 2007, he made an agreement with MIRA Canada to set up MIRA Europe, and three colleagues were sent to Canada to be trained as guide dog instructors.

A new school was a fine idea, but first Frédéric had to find somewhere to put it. Luckily, he didn't have to look far. His grandparents had left him several acres of land that they had used to cultivate vines, peaches, and asparagus, not far from the riverside town of Isle-sur-la-Sorgue. The land was flat and easily accessible, and there was enough of it to accommodate all the necessary facilities.

An architect friend was put to work on designing detailed plans for the school, and Frédéric began looking for financing. Little by little the money was raised, entirely from private and company donations and fund-raisers organized by volunteers. And then, on October 4, 2008, the first stone was laid.

In 2010 and 2011, the instructors came back from Canada, their training completed, and by 2014 the school was finished.

A year or so later, I went to see it for the first time. From what I had heard, it was an extraordinary achievement, all the more extraordinary because it had been done without any financial help at all from the normal official sources. French institutions, for their own obscure reasons, were not in favor of the idea.

I suppose I had been expecting to see something not unlike a barracks—basic, utilitarian, practical. The reality was a delightful surprise. The buildings were simple and modern, the interiors light and airy, the grounds immaculate. On my first visit, I was hoping to meet some dogs, particularly one or two of the St. Pierres—a cross between Labradors and Bernese mountain dogs—that had been specially bred to guide their companions; but it was a period in between school terms, and so I made do instead with some handsome St. Pierre photographs and a detailed account of just what it takes to make a top-class guide dog.

It doesn't come cheap. The cost of training each dog is around 25,000 euros, and even the early part of the process takes a year. This is when the young dogs live with *familles d'accueil*—families that have volunteered to take them in and introduce them to the complexities of living with people, wherever they may go. And these young dogs go everywhere: on trains and buses, up and down busy streets, out to dinner with friends, into shops and cinemas, all the time wearing their first harness, on which is written that they are *chiens en cours d'éducation*. Then, the dogs go to

MIRA at Isle-sur-la-Sorgue, where they are trained by instructors. Only then are they given to the lucky children who become their constant companions. Now it's time for the children to be trained.

They come to the center on several separate occasions. The first is for two days, when they learn all about guide dogs. The second trip lasts a week, when their potential for working with guide dogs is assessed: For instance, do they have a good sense of direction? A good sense of space? Do they have sufficient mobility to be comfortable with their dogs? If these basic checks go well, the children are invited to come back for a month's hand-over program, training and working with their dogs in the busy, complicated world. They take trips on the Métro in Marseille, learning together to take the big leap that must be made to navigate that extra-large step at the end of the escalator. They travel in a car together for the first time. They go shopping. They get a taste of real life as a couple.

Back at the school, a more intense training takes place in the large, beautifully kept area that has been created to give the children and their dogs some familiarity with the complexities they will have to deal with in the streets of towns and cities. These include different surfaces on different levels, different noises, winding pathways, pedestrian crossings, a turnstile, road junctions, raised walkways, part of a badly parked car, a tunnel—an urban jigsaw that stretches for five hundred meters. There are also two fountains and, to educate the nose, clumps of lavender, rosemary, cypress, and roses.

While taking their lessons and getting to know their dogs, the children live at the school, which has a dormitory with ten separate bedrooms, and a spacious living and dining area. At the end of their training, instructors take the children and their dogs back to their homes, where they get used to another, more permanent environment, and where they can work out the routes that they will be using in their new lives, to get to college, for example, or to a friend's house. When school starts, in September, the child, his dog, and his MIRA instructor go together to meet the teachers and the other children, who are taught by the instructor to remember the golden rule of guide dogs: A guide dog is a working unit, not a pet. He is not to be stroked, given tidbits, or otherwise distracted from doing his job. Treats, walks, and affection must wait until his day's work is done, when his harness will be removed and he can relax.

Even after the course has ended, MIRA keeps a close eye on the child and the dog—a kind of after-sales service. This continues for eight years, until the child, now a young adult, can join an adult school and the dog can take his well-earned retirement, often going back to the family he first lived with as a young pup.

On a more recent visit last summer, I was able to go to the school when the new batch of dogs and children were on parade, and I was immediately conscious of the atmosphere. Unlike many places of learning, it was cheerful. There were smiling faces, wagging tails, and a powerful air of optimism as the children began to realize how dramatically their lives were about to be transformed. It was a happy, happy place, and Frédéric should be enormously proud of what he has made possible.

Eighteen

Summer Invasion, Autumn Exodus

$\mathcal{F}$or ten months each year, life in rural Provence is a pleasant succession of tranquil, slow-moving days. There is plenty of time to enjoy friends and to contemplate the meaning of human existence as seen, with a glass of *vin rosé,* from the café terrace. Pressure is reserved for those who live in cities and work in offices, where meetings and appointments dictate the way the days are spent.

This changes every July, when France goes on vacation for two months. Ties and suits give way to shorts and straw hats. Sandwiches at the desk are replaced by three-course lunches with wine. There are walks in the countryside, afternoons by the pool, trips to art galleries and museums, and many other small pleasures that are often neglected because normally there's no time; we're all far too busy.

It's an international complaint, as common among British and Americans as it is among the Belgians, Germans, and Parisians who are part of the summer invasion that takes place in Provence every year to rediscover the joys of a simpler, more relaxed life. How they react to this dose of enforced idleness varies greatly from one nationality to another, and watching these differences has kept me entertained for years.

Leading the way in terms of energy, curiosity, and enthusiasm are the Americans. For them, Provence is a challenge. They can be seen in the café early each morning, plotting the events of the day. Armed with guide books and often with laptops, they calculate times and distances between what they want to see before lunch, where to have lunch, and where to go for the afternoon. The organization is meticulous and the program often quite exhausting, but they have come all the way from Philadelphia and they're damned if they will waste a precious second of vacation time. I always feel they're going to need a few days off when they get back to the States to recover.

I recently asked Monsieur Farigoule if he had any thoughts on our multinational summer visitors. What, for instance, did he think about my fellow Englishmen? His reply to this and my other questions took up most of the morning.

On the whole, he said, the English are acceptable: reasonably well behaved and polite, except when they're having difficulties communicating with anyone who doesn't speak English. This, as they find themselves surrounded by Frenchmen speaking French, frequently leads to what Farigoule described as the Anglo-Saxon counterattack. It starts with a question, delivered in English, often aimed at the café waiter. It could be a request for directions to the café toilet, or an inquiry as to the availability of English beer, but the waiter's response is the same—raised eyebrows, a puzzled expression, and a shrug. Undaunted, the Englishman repeats his question, still in English, but this time a little louder. Then again, louder still. Eventually, the bemused waiter retires to serve someone whose order he can understand.

Englishwomen, on the other hand, are usually much less noisy and more civilized. It's true, said Farigoule, that they have a problem with the tea served in Provençal cafés, which apparently is a poor, insipid copy of the real thing served in England. And they are startled to see their husbands making inroads on the wine as early as ten in the morning. But then, boys will be boys, especially on vacation.

We moved on to consider the German visitors. For them, according to Farigoule, Provence was *"bière et bronzage."* They were always thirsty, always deeply tanned, and always well organized, although not quite up to American standards. As for the Belgians, Farigoule's only observation was one commonly heard in France: they put good French lives at risk because of their habit of driving in the middle of the road.

He was much more vocal about Parisians. "Such arrogance," he said. "Such *snobisme*. They live in their Parisian bubble, and they treat us all like peasants. They look down their noses, they leave miserable tips, they complain about the heat and the prices, they criticize our restaurants. I don't know why they come here. They should stay on the Riviera."

I couldn't believe he was serious. "Surely they can't all be like that?"

"Of course, there are exceptions. I have a dear Parisian friend, and he is one of those exceptions. He is modest, and he has a sense of humor." Unfortunately, one dear Parisian friend clearly couldn't make up for the rest of them. Farigoule was still muttering as he stumped off to lunch.

Recent additions to the list of each year's foreign visitors, whom even Farigoule would approve of, are the Japanese—that is, if he should notice them. I have never seen any clumsy behavior, nor have I ever heard a Japanese shout. When they are gathered around a café table, they chirrup. Otherwise, the loudest noise I have heard them make is the chorus of clicks that comes from their smartphone camera shutters. Noth-

ing can hide from those inquisitive lenses: *boules* players, an artist crouched over his easel, a couple kissing,
a dog slinking off with a stolen *baguette*—every aspect
of village street life seems to fascinate them.

And so the summer season hurries along. But just
when the crowded streets and the flurry of international faces begin to feel permanent, August ends,
September begins, and with almost shocking speed
the crowds are gone. Peace returns. Village inhabitants who have hardly seen one another for two
months once more take possession of the cafés and
restaurants, where they exchange tourist stories and
plans for the coming winter. The early-morning air has
a distinct nip. Scarves and sweaters make a comeback,
and there's a renewed feeling of energy in the village,
almost like a second spring.

Mid-September marks the beginning of the hunting season, when the hills are normally alive with
the sound of gunfire as the hunters flex their trigger
fingers, and all prudent animals make for the more
remote parts of Provence. This year, however, has seen
a significant reduction in the choice of living targets.
The crack-of-dawn fusillades around our house have
all but vanished, and this set me thinking. Has the
price of buckshot tripled? Have pheasants and rabbits
learned to fight back? What could possibly explain the
cease-fire?

I might have known; it was the stomach. A hunter explained, rather sadly, that the wild boar, or *sangliers*, that live in the local forests are not what they used to be. One popular theory is that they have been having carefree romances with ordinary *cochons*, or pigs, and the result is a new breed: the *cochonglier*. This has not been one of nature's triumphs as far as flavor goes. In fact, I am told that the flesh tastes distinctly unpleasant. And, as any good hunter will tell you, if you can't eat it, don't shoot it.

I should add here that this was one hunter's theory rather than a generally held belief, but the fact remains that our Sunday mornings, which used to start with a bang at seven o'clock, are now blessedly peaceful. However, this doesn't mean that the forest is deserted. Furtive figures and their dogs can be seen among the trees pretending to be out for a casual stroll. Far from it, of course—they are hunting for truffles.

There are two powerful traits in the truffle hunter's personality. The first is optimism, the abiding belief that today is the day he will come across a cache of truffles the size of tennis balls. In addition to their market value of more than a thousand dollars a pound, the man who unearths those truffles will find that his reputation will blossom among fellow hunters, who will be convinced that he knows something they don't. And they never will, thanks to the second personality trait: extreme secrecy. A truffle hunter will never tell you exactly where he has found his truffles.

In many ways, this period between September and January is our favorite time of the year. The summer procession of houseguests is over. The village market, while busy, is no longer a scrum. Local restaurants light up their log fires and put thick soups and stews and wild game back on their menus. *Vin rosé* is given a rest, replaced by the full, fresh reds of the region. The village is more spacious without its summer population. And the countryside is a joy—quiet, empty, and beautifully lit by the winter sun, which puts a clean, crisp edge on the rows of clipped vines and the elegant skeletons of leafless trees.

January, when it finally comes, is for many the month to be avoided, either on the ski slopes or by escaping to a warmer climate. It is a cold month, certainly, and occasionally snowy, but I like it. The light is still beautiful, the sky is still a flawless blue, and I always feel that I have the Luberon to myself. There is also, during two or three days each January, a foretaste of warmer times. The temperature goes up by a few degrees, the sun seems a little bigger, and we have fond memories of the occasional January lunch eaten out of doors. Can spring be far behind?

Nineteen

Hollywood Comes to Provence

We first met Ridley Scott more than forty years ago, long before he became Blockbuster Scott. In those days, Jennie and I and Ridley all worked in London, doing our bit for the advertising business; Jennie and Ridley each had TV production companies that specialized in commercials, and I worked as a copywriter in an agency. It was a pretty small universe then, I suppose rather quaint by today's standards, and there was a good deal of mingling. We all knew one another.

My first experience of working with Ridley was on an unpromising project for a deodorant commercial. Try as we might to think of something original to say about it, all traces of originality were weeded out by the client until all we were left with was a tired jingle that had been created by a previous agency to accompany some standard bland footage of young people enjoying themselves.

Even in those days, Ridley had the reputation of being able to make a silk purse out of a sow's ear, and so in desperation we turned to him. At our first meeting, we played the jingle for him. After taking a few moments to recover, he said, "This is a product for young people, right? Let's see what we can do."

And here's what he did. He took the bare bones of the jingle and had it totally remade by one of London's junior rock musicians. He then filmed the band— guitarists, drummer, double-bassist, saxophonists, all of them suitably shaggy and sweaty—playing and singing the jingle. It looked and sounded more like a clip from a televised rock show than a deodorant commercial, and we loved it. So did the client. I've been a fan of Ridley's ever since.

In the years that followed, Ridley went off to Los Angeles and we went off to Provence, where we were pleased and surprised to find one day that we had a distinguished neighbor, none other than Ridley himself, who had a house twenty miles from us. He loved it there, he told us, when he had the chance, but work kept him in LA. So he was permanently on the lookout for something that would let him spend more time in Provence without being gnawed by guilt.

At that time, I was close to finishing a story about a young London executive who inherits a Provençal vineyard from his uncle, and who finds himself up to his neck in grapes and crafty peasants. It was a nice little story, but a long way from the great sweeps of history and drama that Ridley specialized in, and so I was surprised that he asked to see what I'd done. It was more in hope than expectation that I left it with him.

To my surprise, he liked it enough to suggest that I finish it and then let him have another look. So I finished it, he had another look, and that was it. Next stop? Choosing locations and casting. It was that quick.

I knew, of course, that my success was not entirely due to my writing abilities. My story had an unfair advantage over all the other projects that Ridley was considering: it was the only one that offered him the opportunity—no, the obvious necessity—of spending several sunny weeks in his Provençal home.

It didn't take long for news of the film to reach every village in the Luberon, and reactions were mixed. On the whole they were good, with a small chorus of groans and grumbles from those who were convinced that Provence was turning into Disneyland. Despite them, the complex and sometimes delicate preparations for filming went into overdrive: locations had to be found, and terms negotiated. Lodging for cast and crew had to be arranged, transport organized—as I watched, from a safe distance, I began to think that my contribution to the project had been by far the easiest. And then there was the casting.

Ever since the success of *Gladiator*, Ridley had enjoyed a good relationship with Russell Crowe, and so nobody was surprised when he was chosen to play the leading role of the fortunate executive. Naturally, Russell needed to have a little romance as he labored in the vineyard, and here Ridley showed once again his talent for spotting talent. He had given Brad Pitt's career a kick start in *Thelma and Louise*, and this time it was the turn of a young actress, Marion Cotillard, who was then little known outside France. Now, of course, she is a major star. *Merci*, Ridley.

To add the final touches, there was the wonderful Albert Finney, Tom Hollander, and a fine supporting cast. All that remained was to start the cameras rolling.

I had always imagined that shooting a major film would be an exciting, glamorous affair, bursting with high drama and memorable moments. It was high-level showbiz, for heaven's sake, with famous names and delicate egos swirling around. Surely there would be a few social indiscretions at least, if not a full-blooded fight. I got to the set early on the first morning of shooting so I wouldn't miss anything. Marion Cotillard was there, reading a paper. Ridley was having breakfast. Russell was nowhere to be seen. Various technicians scampered back and forth, looking busy and important. The owner of the chateau where we were shooting poked his head out to make sure we weren't trampling on the vines. And that was about as far as the morning's drama went. I was later to find out that Ridley's shoots are like that—extremely well organized, unhurried, and actually quite relaxed. The calm was only disturbed once while I was watching.

This was caused by the star's difficulties with punctuality. Fifteen minutes, twenty minutes, half an hour—Russell seemed to have a problem turning up on time, causing the waiting film crew to sigh loudly and mutter. It wasn't long before they started to call him "the late Russell Crowe," and it might have been this that prompted Ridley to act.

He called a meeting—crew, actors, everybody—to tell them that it was crucial for today's shoot to begin on time. Not a second should be wasted. He wanted a full turnout on set that evening.

Sure enough, they were all there, including Russell. But where was Ridley? They waited. And they waited. And they waited, for forty-five long minutes, until Ridley emerged, apologizing for a long call he'd had to take from LA. After that, the star's punctuality improved significantly.

For me, one of the most memorable scenes in the film was shot in the village of Cucuron, which enjoys the distinction of possessing the biggest *bassin* in Provence—a rectangular, thirty-meter-long ornamental pool, fringed with huge plane trees, the envy of less fortunate villages. On this particular evening, it had been transformed. Tables for two had been placed all the way along the side of the *bassin*, complete with white tablecloths, candles, and fully charged ice buckets. At the far end, a small group of musicians played seductive music, and the surface of the *bassin* was sprinkled with white flowers and floating candles. Magic.

This was the setting for a romantic *diner à deux*, Marion and Russell, alone at last. Well, almost. Because in addition to the crew, a distinguished local figure was studying the idyllic scene. It was his honor the mayor of Cucuron, and he was sufficiently impressed to ask Ridley if there was any chance that the set could be left exactly as it was once shooting was done.

The film was duly finished, but the excitement definitely wasn't over. Cucuron was perhaps the only village in the Luberon to have its own cinema. It was certainly the only village to hold the premiere of a Hollywood movie, and the audience provided a relaxed alternative to the normal premiere crowd.

There was not a limousine or a long dress to be seen, nor a tuxedo. Jackets and jewelry were rare, and pre-screening refreshments were supplied by the local café: *rosé,* and not champagne. The atmosphere was lively, almost boisterous. It was *our* film, and we were going to enjoy it.

The *rosé*-tinged post-screening verdicts were kind, especially from those extras who had spotted themselves decorating various scenes, and the audience eventually drifted off with the feeling of a job well done. The mayor can't wait for Hollywood to call again.

Twenty

Signs of Summer

For most of us, the change in the seasons is a peaceful and often barely noticed affair, marked by gradual differences in temperature, presence or absence of leaves on trees, frosty car windshields, and a dozen other small adjustments to the world around us. In Provence, seasonal change is frequently marked in more dramatic and varied ways, particularly during the delightful period from early spring through to early summer.

Early hints of things to come are the spectacular outbreaks of scarlet poppies in fields that have been quiet and green all winter. The poppies are soon gone, but they stay for long enough to establish a red alert: Put away your heavy clothes, and dust off your espadrilles. Summer's coming.

Slowly at first, but with increasing speed, nature begins to deliver the early examples of its annual show. Among the most spectacular of these are the pink and white billows of almond blossom. At the same time, bare branches develop a green fuzz of foliage, adventurous butterflies emerge to inspect what's going on, the first tentative buds appear, plants that might have been left for dead suddenly start climbing walls again—wherever you look there are small signs of furious activity. And some not-so-small signs as well, from the banks of vivid yellow broom in the fields to the vines, which, although months away from producing grapes, look fresh, green, and promising. In fact, the entire landscape seems to have had a facelift.

This is also the time when the nocturnal orchestra around the house starts rehearsals. Still too early for crickets, but serenades from the tree-frog section begin each evening when the sun goes down. Owls occasionally make a contribution, too, and so one way and another, there is never a dull musical moment.

Meanwhile, down in the village, nature gives way to humanity, with the arrival of the first batch of this year's foreigners, and it may be useful here to explain who fits the local definition of foreigner. In its earliest and most primitive form, a foreigner was someone who wasn't born in the village. Progress has been made since then, and foreigners in Provence are now pretty much the same as foreigners anywhere else. And they are generally well received, partly due

to the sympathy felt by the natives because the foreigner, poor soul, suffers the sad misfortune of not
being French. This sympathy is expressed in a number
of ways, including a significant verbal deceleration,
when the normally hectic pace of Provençal speech
is reduced to a crawl, with the speaker watching anx-
iously to ensure that he's being understood. Or there
is sometimes the ultimate effort: some dusty relics of
elementary English learned at school are brought out,
often with considerable pride. These can be extremely
puzzling. I remember having what I thought was a discussion about the French rugby team's chances when
my companion broke off the conversation, poked my
chest with his finger, and said, in his best English, "I
have a dog. His name is Jules. He likes to walk and
run." There's no answer to that.

The shift in seasons changes the appearance of the
village in a number of ways. Doors to the boutiques are
left open, usually with a chair placed on the pavement
outside so the proprietors can sit in the sun, watch the
world go by, and check out what people are wearing
this year. The village dogs give up the cozy embrace
of their baskets and rediscover the joys of the street—
sights, smells, the chance of stealing a *baguette* from
an unattended shopping basket, and the social and
sporting opportunities offered by the arrival of exotic
tourist dogs visiting from Paris. But the most obvious

change is undoubtedly the rearrangement of the village furniture.

During the chilly winter months, the cafés sharply reduce the number of tables and chairs they allow to stay outside, leaving just a few for the hardy and well-muffled village smokers who are banned from indoor comforts. This changes dramatically, almost overnight, once the temperature has risen.

Previously empty stretches of sidewalk on either side of the main street suddenly sprout café tables and chairs and large umbrellas designed to protect pale-skinned visitors from the sun. The street becomes a rare and welcome example of pedestrians taking precedence over cars. And what a varied bunch they are. On market day you'll see them all—immaculate Parisians, English showing signs of too much sun, Japanese traditionalists and their vintage cameras, Americans with their smartphones, Germans hunting for their next beer, and prematurely weary stallholders who have been up since four a.m. Doing their best to wriggle through this heaving mass with their trays are the waiters and waitresses from the cafés, who have to cross the street to reach their customers. It's bedlam, but a slow-moving, good-humored bedlam, best seen from a well-placed café table.

As you would expect from such a fertile season, there is no shortage of what Monsieur Farigoule likes to describe as "little treasures from God's menu." During the months that pass from May into the true heat of July, there are shorter seasons when you can find the first melons, the first asparagus, the first figs, both green and black, the first and fattest broad beans, plump *petits pois*—all far too fresh to be wearing labels. Instead, they are displayed in shallow wooden trays, and you will often be told that what you buy today was picked earlier that morning. It's enough to put you off supermarket fruits and vegetables for several weeks.

At last, this season in between seasons comes to an end. The temperature climbs, the crickets are in full chirp. It's hot, and going to get hotter. *Bonjour,* summer.

Twenty-One

A Gift from Napoleon

*A*mong Napoleon Bonaparte's memorable achievements, military success would normally take pride of place. Further down the list might be his contribution as a style guru, acknowledging his famous habit of keeping one hand tucked out of sight in his greatcoat. And then, of course, there would be Josephine.

But one Napoleonic addition to *la vie française*, which continues to thrive after more than two hundred years, hasn't received the publicity of his triumphs on the battlefield, or the publicity it deserves. And yet, in its own quiet way, it continues to be an important and, I suspect, well-loved aspect of French society.

It is the Ordre National de la Légion d'Honneur, founded by Napoleon in 1802 to reward outstanding

merit in everyone from industrialists to heroic generals to poets.

What could have prompted Napoleon, not a man
normally known for his good works or social con-
science, to introduce such a wide-ranging and benev-
olent scheme? I've looked in vain for someone or
something that might have inspired him, but in the
absence of any help from history, I've been obliged
to come up with something myself. Here's my theory.

The eighteenth century in France ended with
the Revolution, ten years of bloodshed and turmoil,
marked by the cancellation of all aristocrats and the
execution of Louis XVI in 1793, and only ending when
Napoleon gained power in 1799.

While seen by many as a giant leap of progress, the
Revolution had its critics, many of them senior people
in the military. These were men from good families,
who saw chaos and the destruction of valuable tradi-
tions rather than progress. It was when chatting to
some of his generals during a break between battles
that Napoleon began to realize just how deeply they
had been affected by the fundamental change created
by the Revolution: the elite class had vanished and,
at least for the generals, had left a gaping hole in the
fabric of French life.

Napoleon was sensitive to the moods of his men,

and he was determined, since happy generals made for happy, well-disciplined troops, to make them feel that something would be done to put matters right.

But what?

He ruminated. He pondered. He consulted the histories of the Greek and Roman empires, searching for ideas, until at last inspiration came to him: he would create a new kind of aristocracy—an aristocracy of merit this time, not of birth. Like the army, there would be different ranks, there would be medals, there would be parades and ceremonial events. It would be an honor to belong, and France would once again have its elite. The Légion d'Honneur was born.

Like most foreigners, I had occasionally heard of the Légion d'Honneur, but it wasn't until we were living in France that I began to see a visual sign of its existence. This was elegant and discreet, but difficult to miss: a fine scarlet ribbon sewn into the lapel buttonhole of the jacket. Although no more than a blink of color, it was enough to identify the wearer as a Legionnaire without having to resort to sashes, medals, wigs, or funny hats.

Living, as we were, in the country, jackets were rarely worn, but while on a trip to Paris, glimpses of scarlet on lapels could be seen on every boulevard, and I found myself becoming a lapel snoop.

Once back home, normality returned, until I received a phone call one day from my friend Yves, the mayor of Ménerbes. It was a mysterious call, suggesting that I go out and get a copy of the day's newspaper. When I asked why, the mystery continued. "You'll see," he said. "Read the announcements page. Carefully."

Which I did, and what I saw caused me to spill my glass of *rosé* all over my lap and the café table. I didn't care. I just sat there in my sodden pants, beaming, because there on the page, in black and white, was a list that included my name, informing the world that I was now a Chevalier de la Légion d'Honneur. I must have let out a yelp of excitement, and Paul, the café waiter, came over to see if I needed medical attention. When I told him the news, his eyebrows shot up. *"Ho la la!"* he said, mopping wine from the table. *"Un deuxième verre de rosé?"*

Later, as the euphoria settled down and I gradually became used to the idea of becoming a tiny part of the Légion d'Honneur, I realized how very little I knew about the noble organization—things that every self-respecting Chevalier should know. It was no surprise to find that the Légion, through its members, was involved and influential in many important areas of French life. But what I didn't know was that it owned and administered two of the most distinguished schools in France—La Maison d'Éducation des Loges and La Maison de Saint-Denis. These two schools, originally for orphans who had lost their Legionnaire fathers in battle, had been developed into boarding schools that offered a high-quality education at both elementary and advanced levels for the daughters of Legionnaires. Between them, the two schools take nearly a thousand pupils each year, and their exam results are consistently excellent.

This discovery made it clear to me that the Légion was more than just a ceremonial organization. Behind the ribbons and medals were some serious and extremely worthwhile ideas that were helping to change and improve young people's lives, and so I was more than happy when Yves (who, I learned, was the sponsor responsible for nominating me) suggested that a small celebration should be held to mark my elevation from foreigner to Legionnaire.

It was early summer, and, like all good Provençal celebrations, the event was organized to take place in the open air, in this case on the broad sweep of the terrace in front of the fifteenth-century chateau of Lourmarin.

The sun was shining, the evening sky was postcard blue, and the villagers were out in force. As I looked over the crowded terrace, it seemed to me that almost everyone I had ever met in Provence was there. And not just one, but two mayors—my sponsor, Yves, from Ménerbes, and Blaise Diagne, the mayor of Lourmarin. I had even been given a one-man guard of honor, a local Legionnaire almost entirely concealed behind a giant flag. I was glad I'd worn a suit for the first time in five years.

Yves started off the proceedings by kissing me on both cheeks, saying a few kind words, and pinning the medal of the Légion—my very own medal—onto my waiting chest. And then it was my turn with the microphone.

Making a speech, however brief, in a language not your own is an ordeal. Words you know perfectly well, and have used a hundred times, are forgotten, and in French there is also the added pitfall of gender.

With the formalities out of the way, it was time for serious mingling and the occasional glass of wine. These were the good old days before cell phones had made their assault on face-to-face speech, and I was reminded again of the pleasure the French take in talking to one another. I was also reminded of the difference between the Frenchman and the Englishman when it comes to a simple matter like having a drink.

The Englishman usually treats his alcohol with respect, often cradling his glass in front of him with both hands. The Frenchman would never willingly do this, because he needs his free hand for gesticulation—for tapping the side of his nose for emphasis, for prodding his companion in the chest, squeezing his bicep, patting his cheek, or ruffling his hair. The free hand is necessary for all this, a vital accessory for proper conversation. To watch fifty or more highly animated French people talking at once is like watching a tai chi class on stimulants.

To add to the festivities, Yves had made reservations for a celebratory dinner at a restaurant in the village, and as dusk began to fall we made our way up the narrow street to find our table. There were a dozen of us—two or three American friends, a scattering of English, a solid core of Provençaux, and a couple of Parisians, all feeling merry. Yves warned me not to spill sauce over my newly acquired medal, but apart from that dinner passed in a blur of wine and laughter.

It had been a day to remember. Not for the first time, I blessed the moment we decided to come and live in Provence.

Afterword

Then and Now

*D*uring the summer, I often like to take a seat on the café terrace, pretend to read the newspaper, and eavesdrop. At this time of year I'm surrounded, for the most part, by tourists, and I like to know how they're finding Provence. It's a primitive and highly unreliable form of market research, but I have made one or two interesting discoveries.

By far the most popular topic for those taking part in these café conferences is how Provence has changed from the good old days of their visit the previous year. The price of a cup of coffee, for instance, has gone up yet again, to a giddy three euros. Outrageous. This ignores the fact that for your three euros you get a front-row seat to watch the entertaining spectacle of the village parade for half an hour or so. During that time, you will not be pestered. Nobody will try to sell you more coffee, or tell you that someone else is waiting for your table. Once or twice, I've noticed a customer fast asleep in a corner of the terrace, his beer untouched. He is left to snooze.

It's not only the coffee that has gone up, those visitors say. *Have you seen the price of property around here? And where are those little restaurants with ten-dollar menus? And how about the crowds? I was in Aix yesterday, and I could hardly move. It never used to be like this.*

So it goes on, a lament for a simpler, cheaper, less crowded world that may or may not have existed except in nostalgic memories. What the nostalgians either forget or ignore is that everywhere in the world has been changing, often for the better.

Provence has been spared the worst of the rush into the twenty-first century. There are, of course, new buildings, settlements of livid pink concrete, that have none of the charm of old Provençal architecture. And if you're determined, you can always find a Big Mac, or a magnum of Coca-Cola. Modernity in its various forms is usually available. But people come and come again to Provence for other reasons, most of which haven't changed at all.

Perhaps top of the list is the climate. The sun shines for ten months a year, pausing for the occasional torrent. But when it stops, there is the return of the dense blue sky and diamond-clear light that makes all artists worth their brushes want to get to work.

They have plenty of subjects to choose from. Provence is partly agricultural, with its vines, olives, and melons, partly wild and uninhabited, and partly unashamedly decorative. To see a ten-acre field of lavender in full bloom is to see one of the great sights of summer. And if nature isn't enough, there are dozens of centuries-old villages, often built on hilltops, that are rarely without their artistic admirers in the summer, crouched over their easels, extracting the last picturesque drop from village squares and churches and markets. Everywhere you look, it seems, there is something worth looking at.

Sadly, this does not eliminate the kind of click-and-run tourism that can turn a vacation into an endurance test. These high-speed photographers should relax, and follow the example of the natives of Provence, who are rarely in a hurry. They saunter, rather than run. If you should see a man walking briskly down the village street, consulting his watch and arguing into his cell phone, the chances are that he's either late for lunch or he's a Parisian. For the locals, the day is to be appreciated, taken slowly, and, from time to time, interrupted by a stop at the café. If there were a rating system for the pace of life, Provence would register as "slow."

It's not a bad speed to adopt, because then you won't miss anything. The scenery, of course, is often spectacular. But nature has some stiff competition from the contributions made by man. Roman viaducts and amphitheaters, twelfth-century churches, fifteenth-century bridges, and, one of my favorite places, Marseille. The second-biggest city in France, it was founded in 600 B.C. and hasn't stopped since, with each century leaving its own distinctive mark. There is the Château d'If; the seventeenth-century Vieille Charité, surely the most elegant poorhouse ever built; and, towering above the city, the magnificent Notre-Dame de la Garde, which dates back to the twelfth century. A day in Marseille is like a stroll through history.

This being France, some time has to be made for the stomach. Unlike the more prosperous regions in the north of France, Provence was historically poor. Money was tight, and people ate at home. Going out to a restaurant is a relatively recent luxury, and Provence is still catching up in terms of Michelin stars and world-famous chefs. But in villages like Ansouis and Lourmarin, you can eat simply and well without the ceremonial complications that so often surround good food.

So change is in the air and in the kitchen. But there are many aspects of Provençal life that I hope and trust will stay just as they are today. Here are four of my favorites.

PASTIS

According to a survey I came across recently, the French drink 20 million glasses a day, or roughly 130 million liters a year, of *pastis*. A great part of this is consumed in southeastern France, and it is rare to see a bar or café table anywhere in Provence without a glass or two of it within arm's reach.

I have always found it surprising that a drink of such enormous popularity here in France is barely known in many other countries. Does this indicate, as many have told me, that the taste buds of the Provençal barfly are more finely tuned and sophisticated than lesser taste buds throughout the world? Or is it because *pastis* provides a cooling antidote to the sometimes overenthusiastic use of garlic in Provençal cuisine?

For the answers to questions like this, I am lucky to have my personal professor emeritus of Provençal studies, Monsieur Farigoule, who has been instrumental in helping me to understand many of the curiosities of local life. And so I called him not long ago to ask if he would give me a lesson in *pastis*.

He was waiting at his café table when I arrived,

frowning over a copy of *Le Figaro,* which he pushed away as I sat down. "I hope you're never going to ask me to explain French politicians," he said. He sat back in his chair and sighed. "What a bunch. Where is de Gaulle now that we need him? Right. What's the subject today?" When I told him that I would be grateful for an introduction to *pastis,* he brightened up at once, smiled, nodded, and beckoned to the waiter.

"Pastaga deux fois, sans glaçons." Turning back to me, he said, "First, you must learn the correct way to drink it: no ice cubes. They numb the flavor, and I like to taste what I'm drinking."

The waiter came back and set two narrow, straight-sided glasses of *pastis* on the table next to a miniature jug, which was covered with beads of condensation. Farigoule nodded his approval. "When the jug is sweating, you know that the water is properly chilled." He poured water carefully into the glasses, and we watched the *pastis* turn from brown to a cloudy, milky yellow. *"Bon.* This is how it should be. Like mother's milk for full-grown men."

Although we were drinking Ricard, *"le vrai pastis de Marseille,"* the first sensation was not the shudder and jolt delivered by 45 degrees of alcohol, but a softer, more gentle, and much more pleasant burst of aniseed. Farigoule looked at me, his head cocked. "So?

What do you think? Better than your warm English beer?"

It certainly was. As I said to Farigoule, I was surprised how easily it had slipped down. "That is the little deception of *pastis*," he said. "You think you are drinking an innocent mixture of *anise*, and you forget that the Ricard in your glass contains more alcohol than cognac, vodka, and most whiskies." And with that, he ordered another one for each of us. Never has education tasted so good.

PROVENÇAL TIMING

Ever since we first arrived in Provence, I have been impressed and occasionally mystified by the Provençal methods of dealing with the demands of time in its various forms. Dates and appointments are treated as interesting possibilities rather than commitments, and punctuality should never be taken for granted, except at lunchtime. This is perhaps due to history, when Provence was a truly rural area, and nature was more important than the clock, but old habits die hard. So do old excuses.

Over the years, we have heard some marvelously elaborate reasons to explain why appointments have been delayed or overlooked, why nine o'clock on Monday morning has turned into three thirty on Thursday afternoon. Straightforward apologies are usually avoided. Indeed, anything straightforward is usually avoided. Excuses are complicated, and crammed with distraction and detail. In the end, despite yourself, you feel sorry for the plumber whose aged grandmother has caused him to let you down, the painter who has had his brushes sabotaged by a clumsy assistant, or the electrician whose brain has suffered a power cut, causing him to come to work with equipment that doesn't fit the job (always the supplier's fault).

Another complication is the erratic behavior of the cell phone that everyone in Provence now has. If you should ask why you weren't called to let you know in advance that there was a problem, you will be treated to a menu of minor catastrophes: the phone was destroyed by the family dog; it fell out of a shirt pocket and was drowned in the toilet; it was sent off to the dry cleaners in a pair of pants by mistake; it was confiscated by the *gendarmes* for being used while driving. Rarely can cell phones lead more dangerous lives than they do in Provence.

And yet, despite the inconvenience of missed dates and lengthy delays, I would miss these moments. The ingenuity of the excuses, and the considerable acting skills used by those who invent them, tend to make up for the damage they do to any hopes of a well-ordered life. And when, as does happen from time to time, everything takes place as planned, you feel as though you've won the lottery.

BOULES

Though I've touched on this delightful, leisurely sport earlier, I want to return to it because one of the many charms of this sport is that few can play it really well, *anyone* can play it badly, and everyone can enjoy watching it. Another attraction, for certain players, is that *boules* is one of the very few sporting contests that allow, and sometimes encourage, players to drink while they play. "One hand for the *boule,* and one for the glass" is the advice I was once given. Even the game-changing moment in the history of *boules* is a reminder of the tradition that this is a sport to be played in a relaxed fashion.

Until the early 1900s, *boules* players were obliged to be, if not exactly athletic, at least mobile. *Boule* in hand, they would run up to the throwing line to provide the impetus required to hurl the *boule* toward the *cochonnet,* about twenty meters away. A keen player of this original form of the sport, Jacques le Noir— "Blackie" to his many friends—had been laid low by rheumatism. He could no longer run, and therefore no longer play. But he was still a devoted spectator. And, at heart, still a player.

Most afternoons, a chair would be placed for him at one end of the court, so that he could watch the games in comfort. One day, a close friend, Ernest Pitiot, joined him, standing next to his chair, and the two men decided to start an informal game of their own. Le Noir would throw from a seated position in his chair, and Pitiot, standing next to him, would throw, but with his *pieds tanqués,* feet firmly planted on the ground. This was the birth of modern *boules,* and it immediately appealed to all the older players whose running days were over. Competitions were organized, clubs were formed, the name of the game was changed to *pétanque,* and today the long game is seldom played.

Pétanque is not only for those who play. For me, it is a wonderfully subtle, picturesque game, and to spend an hour or so on a hot summer's evening with dusk setting in, the click of the iron *boules* punctuating the evening chorus of insects, the occasional muffled curse after an unsuccessful throw, and the welcome arrival of a round of drinks—this is my kind of spectator sport.

MARKETS

There is no better cure for supermarket fatigue or shrink-wrap rash than to spend a morning at a Provençal market. Large or small, these markets will restore your faith in shopping—mainly for food, but you never know when you might come across Laguiole knives, hunters' socks, silk scarves, straw hats, or those marvelously imposing pink heavy-duty brassières that have been providing support for generations.

Markets in Provence are said to date from the twelfth century, when farmers and craftsmen gathered every week to sell what they had grown or made, and this basic function still survives. But the market today is much more than a purely practical supply service. It has become a social hub, often the setting for a little light musical entertainment from visiting troubadours, and, along with the cafés, gossip headquarters for the village.

The market day begins early—by eight o'clock the stalls are set out, with the stallholders chatting with one another while they put the finishing touches to their displays. And here you can see the first and most obvious difference between market and supermarket: the absence of packaging. What you see laid out on the market stalls is produce that was picked the day before—lettuce, peaches, potatoes, cherries, grapes, the occasional immense squash, newly laid eggs—all neatly arranged, without a brand name or a trademark to be seen anywhere. The experienced market shopper will always be equipped with something in which to carry the purchases home, because the best you'll get from the stallholder to hold what you buy will be a modest brown paper bag.

As you walk through the stalls, you will come across small knots of people, cheerful and animated, who give the impression that they are old friends who haven't seen each other for years. They chatter, they giggle, they occasionally whisper, and it's hard to believe that they have been living next door to one another for years in the same village street. But such is the magic of the latest dubious piece of gossip that it invigorates the entire group.

And so on you go, past the fragrant cheese truck, past the mobile fresh fish emporium, and the baker with his two-foot-long loaves of warm brown bread, until you reach a much larger group, who are sampling one of the specialties that show up in the market from time to time.

This year's novelty is the *FoieGrasBurger,* and early reports say that it is an exotic experience, certainly not to be confused with more conventional members of the burger family. Will it take America by storm? Will it inspire more burger refinements? Can we expect one day to see the CaviarBurger?

Eventually, around one o'clock, the stallholders

start to pack up, their job done. It's all over, until next week. Once again, baskets have been filled with good things to eat. And once again, the stomach will be served.

I must go. Lunch is calling.

ALSO BY

PETER MAYLE

PROVENCE A–Z
A Francophile's Essential Handbook

Provence A–Z is the ultimate "dictionary" for lovers of
Provence: Peter Mayle's personal selection of the foods,
customs, and words he finds most fascinating, curious,
delicious, or just plain fun. Though organized from A
to Z, this is hardly a conventional work of reference. In
more than 170 entries, Peter Mayle writes about subjects
as wide-ranging as architecture and *zingue-zingue-zoun* (in
the local patois, a word meant to describe the sound of a
violin). And, of course, he writes about food and drink:
vin rosé, truffles, olives, melons, bouillabaisse, the cheese
that killed a Roman emperor, even a cure for indigestion.
Provence A–Z is a delight and the perfect complement to
any guidebook on Provence or, for that matter, France.

Travel/Humor

FRENCH LESSONS
Adventures with Knife, Fork, and Corkscrew

The French celebrate food and drink more than any other
people, and Peter Mayle shows us just how contagious
their enthusiasm can be. We visit the Foire aux Escargots.
We attend a truly French marathon, where the beverage of
choice is Château Lafite Rothschild rather than Gatorade.
We search out the most pungent cheese in France and eavesdrop on a heated debate over the perfect way to prepare
an omelet. We even attend a Catholic mass in the village
of Richerenches, a sacred event at which thanks are given
for the aromatic, mysterious, and breathtakingly expensive
black truffle. With Mayle as our charming guide, we come
away satisfied (if a little hungry) and with a sudden desire
to book a flight to France at once.

Travel/Food

ENCORE PROVENCE
New Adventures in the South of France

Mayle gives us a glimpse into the secrets of the truffle trade, a parfumerie lesson on the delicacies of scent, an exploration of the genetic effects of two thousand years of foie gras, and a small-town murder mystery that reads like the best fiction. Here, too, are Mayle's tips on where to find the best honey, cheese, or chambre d'hôte the region has to offer. Lyric, insightful, and sparkling with detail, *Encore Provence* brings us to a land where the smell of thyme in the fields or the glory of a leisurely lunch is no less than inspiring.

Travel

TOUJOURS PROVENCE

Peter Mayle offers us another deliciously evocative book about life in Provence. With tales only one who lives there could know—finding gold coins while digging in the garden, indulging in sumptuous feasts at truck stops—and with characters introduced with great affection and wit—the gendarme fallen from grace, the summer visitors ever trying the patience of even the most genial Provençaux, the straightforward dog "Boy"—*Toujours Provence* is a heartwarming portrait of a place where, even if you can't quite "get away from it all," you can have a very good time trying.

Travel

A YEAR IN PROVENCE

In this witty and beautiful account, Peter Mayle tells what it is like to realize a long-cherished dream and actually move into a two-hundred-year-old stone farmhouse in the remote country of the Lubéron with his wife and two large dogs. He endures January's frosty mistral as it comes howling down the Rhône Valley, discovers the secrets of goat racing through the middle of town, and delights in the glorious regional cuisine.

Travel

THE DIAMOND CAPER

When a Riviera socialite's diamonds are stolen—the latest in a string of seemingly unconnected but increasingly audacious jewelry heists across France—Peter Mayle's bon vivant and master sleuth, Sam Levitt, and his partner, Elena Morales, are soon on the case. In these "perfect crimes," Sam sees the hand of a master criminal, but as he and Elena dig deeper, they begin to realize just how dangerous it may be to pursue the truth. In the midst of all the excitement, there's a house to renovate, rosé to share, and feasts of the Provençal summer bounty to enjoy—giving *The Diamond Caper* all the hallmarks of another delightfully sun-splashed Peter Mayle adventure.

Fiction

THE CORSICAN CAPER

When billionaire Francis Reboul finds himself on the wrong side of a Russian tycoon, he's fortunate to have vacationing friends Sam Levitt and Elena Morales on hand to help him out. Now it's up to Sam—who's saved Reboul's neck before—to negotiate with an underworld of mercenaries, hit men, and mafiosi, to prevent his friend from becoming a victim of "Russian diplomacy." As usual, Sam and Elena still find time to enjoy the good life, but as Sam's sleuthing draws him closer to the truth, he realizes Reboul might not be the only one in trouble. Rich with clever twists, sparkling scenery, and mouthwatering gustatory interludes as only Peter Mayle can write them, *The Corsican Caper* is an adventure par excellence.

Fiction

THE MARSEILLE CAPER

When lovable rogue and sleuth extraordinaire Sam Levitt's last adventure in France ended, he thought it'd be awhile before he was back, especially with the beautiful Elena Morales to keep him in Los Angeles. But a job offer from the immensely wealthy Francis Reboul soon has Sam and Elena in sunny Marseille on a quest for further excitement—and delectable dining. Yet as competition over the valuable local waterfront grows more hotly disputed, Sam, representing Reboul, finds himself in the middle of an increasingly intrigue-ridden and dangerous real estate grab.

Fiction

THE VINTAGE CAPER

The Vintage Caper begins high above Los Angeles with a world-class heist at the impressive wine cellar of lawyer Danny Roth. Enter Sam Levitt, former lawyer and wine connoisseur, who follows leads to Bordeaux and Provence. The unraveling of the ingenious crime is threaded through with Mayle's seductive renderings of France's sensory delights—from a fine Lynch-Bages to the bouillabaisse of Marseille—guaranteed to charm and inform even the most sophisticated palates.

Fiction

A GOOD YEAR

Max Skinner has recently lost his job at a London financial firm and just as recently learned that he has inherited his late uncle's vineyard in Provence. On arrival he finds the climate delicious, the food even better, and two of the locals ravishing. Unfortunately, the wine produced on his new property is swill. Why then are so many people interested in it? Enter a beguiling Californian who knows more about wine than Max does—and may have a better claim to the estate. Fizzy with intrigue and bursting with local color and savor, *A Good Year* is Peter Mayle at his most entertaining.

Fiction

Once upon a time in Provence, Peter Mayle adopted a dog of uncertain origin and dubious hunting skills and gave him a name—Boy. Now he gives this canny canine a voice in an irresistible "memoir" that proves that the best vantage point for observing life may well be on all fours. As Boy recounts his progress from an overcrowded maternal bosom to unchallenged mastery of the Mayle household, he tells us why dogs are drawn to humans ("our most convenient support system") and chickens ("that happy combination of sport and nourishment"). We share in his amorous dalliances, his run-ins with French plumbers and cats, and the tidbits (both conversational and edible) of his owners' dinner parties. Enhanced by fifty-nine splendidly whimsical drawings by Edward Koren, *A Dog's Life* gives us all the delights we expect from any book by Peter Mayle—pedigree prose, biting wit, and a keen nose for the fragrance of civilization—together with the insouciant wisdom of which only a dog (and probably only Peter Mayle's dog) is capable.

Fiction/Pets

HOTEL PASTIS
A Novel of Provence

Simon Shaw, a rumpled, fortyish English advertising executive, has decided to leave it all behind and head off to France to transform an abandoned police station in the Lubéron into a small but world-class hotel. On his side, Simon has a loyal majordomo and a French business partner who is as practical as she is ravishing. But he hasn't counted on the malignant local journalist—or on the mauvaise types who have chosen the neighboring village as the site of their latest bank robbery. Slyly funny and overflowing with sensuous descriptions of the good life, *Hotel Pastis* is the literary equivalent of a four-star restaurant.

Fiction

CHASING CÉZANNE

Hanky-panky on the international art scene is the source of the hilarity and fizz in *Chasing Cézanne*. Mayle flies us back to the South of France on a wild chase through galleries, homes of prominent collectors, and wickedly delectable restaurants. Andre Kelly, sent to Cap Ferrat to take glamorous photographs of the houses and treasures of the rich, famous, and fatuous, happens to have his camera at the ready when he spots a Cézanne being loaded onto a plumber's truck near the home of an absent collector. *Odd*, thinks Andre. And in no time he's on the trail of a state-of-the-art scam, chasing Cézanne.

Fiction

ANYTHING CONSIDERED

In Provence, a suave if slightly threadbare English expat named Bennett is reaching the end of his credit. In desperation he places an ad in the *International Herald Tribune*: "Unattached Englishman . . . seeks interesting and unusual work. . . . Anything considered except marriage." In no time at all Bennett is being paid handsomely to impersonate the mysterious and very wealthy Julian Poe. This entails occupying Poe's palatial flat in Monte Carlo, whizzing around in his Mercedes, and charging meals at the Côte d'Azur's better restaurants. Unfortunately, there are certain complications involving Sicilian and Corsican mafiosi, the loveliest woman ever to drive a tank, and a formula for domesticating the notoriously unpredictable black truffle. These elements make *Anything Considered* a novel of nail-biting suspense and champagne-dry wit, whose evocations of the good life are so convincing, you'll come away with a suntan.

Fiction

VINTAGE DEPARTURES & VINTAGE BOOKS
Available wherever books are sold.
www.vintagebooks.com